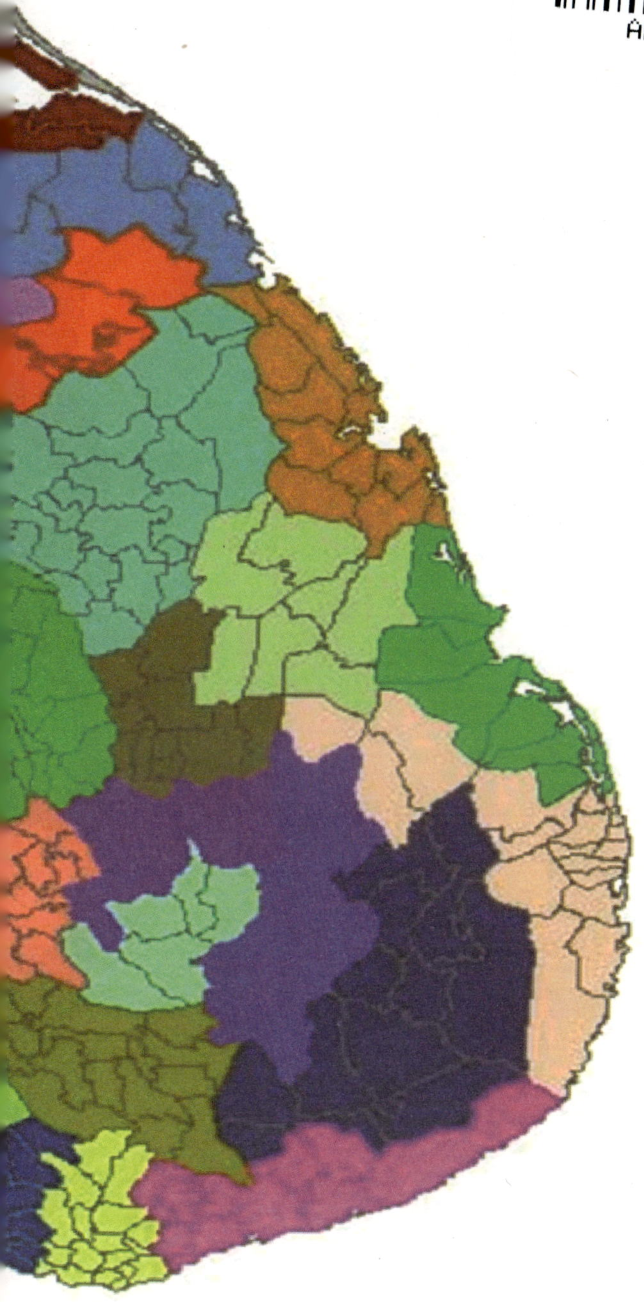

Looking Beyond the Conflict

Changing Dynamics of India-Sri Lanka Ties

Looking Beyond the Conflict

Changing Dynamics of India-Sri Lanka Ties

Rajeswari Pillai Rajagopalan
N. Sathiyamoorthy
K. Yhome
Rahul Prakash
Wilson John

OBSERVER RESEARCH FOUNDATION

HAR-ANAND
PUBLICATIONS PVT LTD

This study has been prepared by the Observer Research Foundation. It has been adapted from a work submitted to the Integrated Defence Staff, Ministry of Defence, in April 2012.

Published by Ashok Gosain and Ashish Gosain for:
HAR-ANAND PUBLICATIONS PVT LTD
E-49/3, Okhla Industrial Area, Phase-II, New Delhi-110020
Tel: 41603490 Fax: 011-41708607
E-mail: haranand@rediffmail.com/info@haranandpublications.com
Website: www.haranandpublications.com

Printed in India at Vinayak Offset

About the Authors

RAJESWARI PILLAI RAJAGOPALAN is a Senior Fellow at the Observer Research Foundation (ORF), New Delhi. Dr. Rajagopalan joined ORF after an almost five-year stint at the National Security Council Secretariat (2003-2007), where she was an Assistant Director. Prior to joining the NSCS, she was Research Officer at the Institute of Defence Studies and Analyses, New Delhi. She was also a Visiting Professor at the Graduate Institute of International Politics, National Chung Hsing University, Taichung, Taiwan in early 2012. Her areas of research include Indian and Asian foreign policy and security issues, U.S. foreign policy, space security and other arms control issues, Sri Lankan politics, and ethnic conflicts. She has authored three books and co-authored and contributed to several books and policy reports.

N. SATHIYAMOORTHY is Director, Observer Research Foundation – Chennai Chapter. He is a widely travelled journalist with expertise on Sri Lanka, Maldives, and issues related to Indian politics and elections. His articles are published regularly in India and abroad.

K. YHOME is a Research Fellow at the Observer Research Foundation (ORF), New Delhi. His research interests include India's neighbourhood policy, China's southwestern Provinces, the South China Sea, the Bay of Bengal, regionalism and sub-regionalism in South and Southeast Asia. Recently, his research has focused on the political changes in Myanmar and the changing geopolitical dynamics in the Bay of Bengal region.

RAHUL PRAKASH is a Junior Fellow at Observer Research Foundation (ORF), New Delhi. His research interests include technology and security, Chemical, Biological, Radiological and Nuclear (CBRN) issues and security developments in Asia. He has co-authored a report on "Chemical, Biological and Radiological Materials: An Analysis of Security Risks and Terrorist Threats in India," an outcome of a joint study conducted by ORF and the London-based Royal United Services Institute. He has also published issue briefs on China's progress in outer space and rise of microblogs in China.

WILSON JOHN is a Senior Fellow and Vice President at the Centre for International Relations at Observer Research Foundation (ORF), New Delhi. His interests include the South Asian geopolitics, asymmetric warfare, Islamist extremism, and civil-military relations. He is recognised as one of the leading authorities on the militant group, Lashkar-e-Tayyeba. He has authored/edited 11 books on issues of security and terrorism.

Other Contributors

We are grateful to Kaustav Chakrabarti, Sadhavi Chauhan, P.K. Ghosh, Sripathi Narayanan, Uma Purushothaman, Vivan Sharan and Akhilesh Variar for contributing to the research and content of the report. We remain also thankful to Daniel Rubin and Avinash Paliwal for their painstaking effort in editing the manuscript.

Executive Summary

India's relationship with Sri Lanka should be defined by two key strategic objectives: ensuring the sovereignty and integrity of the island nation, even as India seeks a durable political solution acceptable to all sides; and preventing any external player with interests inimical to India's own from gaining a foothold in Sri Lanka. In pursuing these goals, New Delhi has to contend with its own limitations and compulsions.

The major challenge for India in dealing with Colombo comes from within, particularly the 'Tamil Nadu factor.'[1] Additionally, India lacks a long-term strategic plan aimed at forging a strong partnership with Sri Lanka, an important littoral nation of the Indian Ocean Region (IOR). This region remains vital for India as an emerging global power. Consequently, after nearly three decades of ethnic conflict, the current situation and future outlook in Sri Lanka presents important challenges and opportunities for India.

EMERGING TRENDS

POLITICAL TRENDS

Post-war Sri Lankan politics are changing dramatically. There is an apparent movement towards a more inclusive political

[1]Tamil Nadu is only a few kilometres from the coast of Sri Lanka and the Tamil-speaking north and east. Considerable support and sympathy exists among Dravidian political parties and leaders for the Sri Lankan Tamils. This factor has, from time to time, impacted India's Sri Lanka policy.

environment. Correlated, the new political landscape is dominated by coalition politics fuelled by vote-bank considerations. These new dynamics may even allow minority ethnic parties, including Tamil parties, to join the national political system.

Moreover, a generational transition from older elitist politicians to today's leaders—who belong to different strata of society—will introduce new-found regional, caste and class representation to the political scene. Ideally, this will open political space for minorities and other social strata. A likely demographic shift towards Muslims in the eastern province may also shift the minority political calculus, perhaps meaning Muslim minority political domination at the cost of other ethnic groups, particularly the Tamils.

However, it remains unlikely that Sri Lanka's centrist and sectarian nature will undergo dramatic shifts in the coming years. The aforementioned possibilities have yet to take root, and will continue to be shaped and influenced by other factors. The pace and seriousness of the rehabilitation, reconstruction, and ethnic reconciliation efforts initiated by the Sri Lankan government will determine to a great extent the new political dynamics. At first blush, governmental efforts on these fronts appear inadequate. Additionally, demobilising a large military and finding alternative career opportunities for soldiers is difficult and of great concern in terms of maintaining the army's traditional, apolitical nature. These issues will play a role in determining the country's future political character.

SECURITY TRENDS

With the end of the war, Sri Lanka is unlikely to face the same internal security threats formerly posed by the LTTE. However, absent political and social solutions, resurgent Tamil nationalism is likely. Radicalisation of the Muslim community in the Eastern Province may also jeopardise internal security. Given its history, the Sri Lankan government will not shy away from crushing any armed resistance from either community at its inception.

Externally, Sri Lanka is unlikely to face a major security threat absent major balance of power unrest in the IOR. However, Sri Lankan action, such as providing a military base for China, would risk irking India, the U.S., and other powers with significant IOR stakes.

GEOPOLITICAL TRENDS IN THE IOR

Asia Pacific geopolitical dynamics are rapidly changing. Principally, China is rising, and rivalry among major IOR powers is increasing. In this backdrop, Sri Lanka's strategic location at the crossroads of every major maritime route in the region gives the country major significance in the strategic calculus of India and other external powers operating in the area.

Recognising its location-aided advantage, Sri Lanka plans to develop its port, air, road, and rail infrastructure, strengthening its regional connectivity with the hope of becoming a major transit hub. These developments may attract major players to increase their foothold in the island nation.

IOR rivalries, for example, between India and China are intensifying, with both countries trying to woo Indian Ocean littoral states with investments and concessional loans for development. During the war and post-war period, Sri Lanka has played this rivalry for its own gain. China's likely increased IOR presence may subsequently prompt other powers, such as the U.S., to increase their level of engagement with Colombo in an effort to counter-balance China's clout.

Economic globalization has had a manifold effect in enhancing seaborne trade, as 70 per cent of the global oil trade and 50 per cent of container traffic pass through various Indian Ocean choke points. Seventy percent of India's trade, 80 per cent of China's oil, and 90 per cent of China's overall trade passes through this region.

While benefitting economically, Colombo is likely to find itself at the centre of major power interests and competition. Colombo's subsequent balancing act will likely determine its future role in emerging IOR geopolitics. Given Sri Lanka's Indian proximity and India's rising geopolitical and military power, Colombo will need to tread carefully, restraining itself from crossing certain red lines vis-à-vis India.

ECONOMIC TRENDS

The Sri Lankan economy has witnessed steady growth since 2002. In the post-war era, Sri Lanka must sustain high growth in order to meet its many needs. These include: the growing aspirations of its people; reconstructing war-torn areas; and becoming South Asia's transit hub. Under these circumstances, economic compulsions are likely to drive Colombo's internal and external policies.

Despite high growth, Sri Lanka's economic progress continues to face internal and external obstacles. As a key piece of Sri Lanka's high growth puzzle, the service sector has been strengthened by government efforts aimed at making its services exportable and resistant to international competition. Government support for the development of ports, aviation, energy, knowledge, and commercial trading and banking/finance suggest that the already prospering service sector may further improve and pull-up the country's economy.

Another drag on Sri Lanka's economy is its weapons and artillery payment obligations acquired during the LTTE war. This is expected to continue squeezing the Sri Lankan treasury over the next few years.

In order to sustain the economy's upward trajectory, it must become more inclusive. For example, while women of working age far outpace men, a large proportion of this female labour force remains unemployed. Furthermore, the agricultural sector contributes far less to overall GDP as compared to the percentage of people it employs, reflecting the need to gainfully utilise people employed in this sector.

As the Sri Lankan service sector continues to develop in the coming years (supplemented by continued foreign aid and investments), the country's GDP will accelerate. However, the social benefits from enhanced government revenue will depend on the composition of the government in power. While Sri Lanka's economic situation has improved in recent years, there remain several obstacles to fulfilling its 'emergent Singapore' ambitions by 2025.

In the short run, political pressure from the international community is unlikely to alter the flow of foreign investments and assistance flowing to Sri Lanka's economy. Crucial economic partners continue to support Colombo so far. However, in the long run, Sri Lanka must ensure effective implementation of the Lessons Learnt and Reconciliation Commission (LLRC) recommendations if it wants to maintain the same or accelerate external assistance and funds.

TRENDS IN INDIA-SRI LANKA RELATIONS

India remains committed to the sovereignty, unity, and integrity of Sri Lanka. This commitment was clearly exhibited by India's restrained position during the Sri Lankan offensive against the LTTE, despite valid humanitarian concerns. As a result, nascent common ground and mutual trust has been developed.

New Delhi's non-intervention approach was the surest sign to Colombo that India intends to deliver on its commitment to strengthen bilateral ties, a commitment soon put to test. India's vote against Sri Lanka at the United Nations Human Rights Council (UNHRC) two years in a row has upset Colombo. The Geneva vote has yet again proven that the relationship is still driven by internal domestic issues and compulsions on both sides.[2]

[2]The United Nations Human Rights Council passed a resolution in 2012, sponsored by the U.S., arguing for greater reconciliation and accountability by the Sri Lankan government. India was among the 24 countries that voted against Sri Lanka whereas 15 countries—including China, Russia and other South Asian countries—voted against the resolution. See "India Votes Against Sri Lanka, UN Human Rights Council Resolution Adopted," *NDTV*, March 22, 2012, available at http://www.ndtv.com/article/world/india-votes-against-sri-lanka-un-human-

While New Delhi is aware of Sri Lanka's relations with external players, including China and Pakistan, India's inability to strike a balance between its domestic political compulsions and strategic interests in Sri Lanka will remain a challenge in coming years. Sri Lanka's questionable record on human rights issues relating to war crimes is unlikely to disappear in the near future. Even as economic and defence ties between the two countries have increased, there is definite scope for further improvement.

It is important to recognise that China's efforts at deepening engagement with Sri Lanka may not translate into military benefits for Beijing. The geographical distance and the enormous investment in infrastructure and capability needed to create a Chinese military anchor in Sri Lanka will continue to be strong deterrents. Consequently, it would behove India neither to over-estimate China's influence in Sri Lanka, nor to let it dominate New Delhi's relationship with Colombo. New Delhi's ability to craft an innovative foreign policy vis-à-vis Sri Lanka by removing the dichotomy in its relations with Colombo and rationally analysing the involvement of external actors will determine the depth and direction of bilateral economic and defence ties.

SRI LANKA IN 2025

Scenario I: Sinhala-Majority, yet Coalition Government

Sri Lanka's political landscape is expected to be characterised by more continuity than change. The current political dynamics and party formations are not likely to show any major changes. The major political parties, such as the SLFP and the UNP, will remain

rights-council-resolution-adopted-188871. India voted for a second time at the UNHRC against Sri Lanka in 2013. 25 countries voted against Sri Lanka and 13 countries, including Pakistan, voted for Sri Lanka, while eight member-states abstained from voting on the resolution. See "India Votes Against Sri Lanka at UNHRC, DMK Slams Govt. for Diluting Resolution," *The Times of India,* March 21, 2013, available at http://articles.timesofindia.indiatimes.com/ 2013-03-21/india/37902646_1_llrc-unhrc-sri-lanka.

at the helm of Sri Lanka's political affairs, as it appears no opposing political force will challenge their dominance. The relatively moderate mainstream political parties are likely to dominate politics in the near future. However, given the trend toward coalition politics, changing patterns of political alliances will bring even smaller, ethnically-based minority parties to the fore.

Colombo's ambitions for regional trade hub status will provide India with attractive policy options. New Delhi should take advantage of its geographical proximity, history of close association, and shared heritage by providing significant financial assistance and technical support.

However, India's foreign policy challenges are likely to remain. India must balance two developments. First, India's domestic political compulsions would dictate speedy ethnic reconciliation, but it must balance this desire with another to minimise the influence of countries whose interests are inimical to its own, such as China and Pakistan.

Scenario II: A Pluralistic Sri Lankan Government

The main drivers engendering this scenario are political, ethno-religious and demographic. This scenario can only occur when Sri Lanka's ethnic and religious minorities are given an equal political platform and they begin to emerge as influential powers in Sri Lankan polity. Two primary factors may allow this:

- Current and future Colombo regimes succumb to international pressure—making serious efforts at ethnic reconciliation, addressing the issues faced by the country's minorities and providing them political space. Additionally, equal opportunities in education, employment, and social development (especially in the North and East) are necessary.
- Given the likely persistent trend towards coalition politics, minority party coalition members may tip the balance in

forming governments. In such a scenario, the government would have to consider minority party demands in order to sustain their support.

Sri Lanka's aggressive efforts to develop itself as a major transit point for international shipping, presenting a cheaper alternative to Singapore, are increasingly being noticed by the international community. It cannot be overemphasised that Colombo's trade-hub ambitions provide India with immense geopolitical opportunity. Accordingly, India should extend all support to Sri Lanka, including technical and financial.

Scenario III: Majoritarian Sinhala Government

If Sri Lankan society and government fail to recover from their current triumphalism, the Sinhala-majority parties could harden their stance against the country's minority communities. Amidst fears of a resurgence of LTTE-like groups—a fear prevalent among the Sinhalese—the government may adopt policies aimed at enhancing its stronghold over Tamils and Muslims. This is reflected in the government's development policies that ignore the Northern and Eastern Provinces.

Uneven national development may fuel discontent, becoming a contributing factor to minority resurgence against the Sinhala-Buddhist state. The short-term consequence of the government's approach will be growing dissatisfaction within minorities about being excluded from national development. If the government continues this policy longterm, polarisation along ethno-political lines (between the Sinhalese Buddhist majority and minority Tamil and Muslim communities) will only widen.

This could feed into the possible revival of Tamil nationalism. These factors may push the country to a situation where Sinhala right-wing parties return to power. Internally, such a scenario will have an adverse political impact. However, this right-wing government may enjoy significant external support from players like China. This may embolden the government to curb minority community development.

The marginalisation of Tamil society becomes a concern for India due to domestic politics, i.e., 'Tamil Nadu factor.' India might have to deal with Tamil migration from Sri Lanka, which will, in turn, create refugee housing and employment problems for New Delhi. Given China's increasing engagement with Sri Lanka, New Delhi will be compelled to maintain good relations with Colombo.

SRI LANKA – AT A GLANCE

Population: 20.87 million; growth rate: 0.9 %

Area: 65,610 sq. km

Capital: Colombo

Head of Government: President Mahinda Rajapaksa (Sri Lankan Freedom Party)

Ethnic Groups: Sinhala (75.88%); Sri Lankan Tamils (11.21%); Indian Tamils (4.16 %); Moors (9.23 %); Burghers (0.18%); Malays (0.20%)

Languages: Sinhala (74%); Tamil (18%); Others (8%)

Religions: Buddhists (70.19%); Hindus (12.61%); Muslims (9.71%); Christians (7.45%); Others (0.05%)

Life Expectancy at Birth: 74.9

Literacy: 90.7 % (Male: 91.9%; Female: 90.8%)

Sectoral Contribution to GDP (% of GDP): Agriculture: 12.1%; Industry: 29.9%; Services: 58.0%

GDP (annual change in %): 8.3 %; Agriculture: 1.5%, Industry: 10.3%; Services: 8.6%

Inflation (at Consumer prices): 6.7 %

Labour Force: 7429.79 million; Agriculture: 2445.25 million; Industry: 1841.44 million; Services: 3143.10 million

Unemployment (in numbers and %): 307.95 million; 4.0%
Exports: $9.37 billion

Destination of Exports: EU (33.0%); U.S. (21.7%); UK (10.8%); Middle East (10.1%); India (5.8%)

Imports: $16.89 billion

Source of Imports: India (19.0%); China (13.9%); Singapore (8.8%); UAE (6.7%); Malaysia (4.2%)

Defence Expenditure (2012): $1.54 billion (2.4% of GDP)

Source: Asian Development Bank; CIA, *The World Factbook;* Department of Statistics and Census, Government of Sri Lanka; Central Bank of Sri Lanka.

Contents

I

Introduction
A Brief Historical Overview

India-Sri Lanka relations date back more than 2,500 years. Both warring ethnic groups—the majority Sinhala and the minority Sri Lankan Tamils—trace their lineage to India. A majority of the Sinhalese also identify as Buddhists, tracing their lineage to Prince Mahendra and Princess Sangamitra, known in Sinhala as Mahinda and Sangamitta.[3] These were the son and daughter of Emperor Ashoka. The pupil tree—or *bo* tree, as known in Sri Lanka and worshipped with great reverence at holy Buddhist shrines in Kandy—is said to have been brought by the princess. Cultural relations between Indians and Sri Lankans have remained very close, with the native Sri Lankan Tamils visiting Hindu temples in Tamil Nadu on pilgrimage. Pilgrimage sites include ones at Madurai, Palani, and Tiruchendur. For the Buddhists of Sri Lanka, worshipping at Bodh Gaya, Sarnath, and other centres across northern India is a lifetime vow for attaining salvation.

However, historical ethnic divides in Sri Lanka make ties to India region-specific. The seeds of ethnic conflict in Sri Lanka were sown in the island's ancient and medieval history, not merely through the 1956 'Sinhala Only' law, as often thought. The Sinhalese have not forgiven Tamils for the Chola King Rajaraja's capture of their thousand year-old kingdom—one of the reasons for

[3]Mithra Fernando, "Myth and Fantasy of the Sinhalas," *Lankan News Papers*, March 28, 2009, available at http://www.lankanewspapers.com/news/2009/3/41581_space.html (accessed on December 05, 2011).

mistrust. The Tamils have historically believed the episode fitting revenge for the defeat of septuagenarian King Ellara by a youthful Duttegemunu another thousand years earlier. This event was chronicled in the *Mahavansa*, a Sinhala-Buddhist epic dating to the sixth century. The *Mahavansa* also speaks of an Indian King, Vijaya, landing on a ship in Sri Lanka and marrying a local tribal woman. According to this epic, his progeny would come to rule the island.

Sinhala-Buddhist literature also talks about the 'destruction' wrought by the Chola enterprise. Ethnic animosity was handed down from generation to generation, with each century adding a new, divisive dimension to the picture. In the post-independence era, since the late 1940s, the animosity between the Sinhala majority and the Sri Lankan Tamil minorities has been fuelled by school textbooks, which teach non-secular post-colonial history. In fact, the choice of the Cholas' Tiger emblem as the symbol of the Liberation Tigers of Tamil Eelam (LTTE), founded in the 1970s, has a deeper meaning than ordinarily understood. It was not a reference to Indian assistance to Sri Lankan Tamils aimed at fending off constitutional inequities but a reflection of revived glory under Rajaraja Chola. All post-independence ethnic conflicts carry extreme historical baggage, making predictable and inefficient solutions all too likely.

COLONIAL HISTORY

Variously called 'Serendeep' or 'Ceylon' by travellers and conquerors, Sri Lanka was subjected to colonial rule for several centuries before attaining independence in 1948. Sri Lanka's colonial history can be traced to its first European visitors, the Portuguese, in 1505. They were followed by the Dutch and the British, who consolidated their footprint in Ceylon in early 19th century. The British introduction of tea and rubber plantations to Ceylon made the rich colony a source of wealth for the Empire. Labour needed for the plantation was met by an influx of Indian

(Tamil)[4] indentured labour, since the local population was unwilling to forego traditional agricultural practices. These Tamil-speaking labourers were brought in large numbers and constituted a sizeable chunk of the population.

Over time, British colonisers favoured certain sections of the population, particularly the Tamils (Sri Lankan), for government employment, which included bureaucracy and other state-privileged sectors like education. This group was predominantly concentrated in the northern areas of the country. Preferential treatment by the British sowed the seeds of discontent among sidelined sections of society and would eventually give birth to the ethnic conflict that later gripped Sri Lanka for more than three decades. Their fortunes further changed with the arrival of American-Jesuit missionaries aiming to spread religion, education and healthcare. These efforts soon produced clerks for the British rulers, whereas the European-based education in the South turned Sinhala elite onto the Ox-Bridge model in large numbers.[5]

STRATEGIC LOCATION

Given its strategic location, Ceylon played a crucial Asian theatre role during the Second World War, serving as Allied headquarters towards the end of the war. Then post-war, anti-colonial wave took root in Ceylon too, resulting in the British relinquishing their final toehold on the Indian Subcontinent in February 1948. However, it took another decade—and the election of a centre-left government under Prime Minister SWRD Bandaranaike in 1956—for Sri Lanka to attain British acquiescence in relinquishing the Royal Air Force (RAF) Kattunayake base. Additionally, the British also let go

[4]Daniel Naujoks, "Emigration, Immigration, and Diaspora Relations in India," *Migration Policy Institute,* available online at http://www.migrationinformation.org/feature/display.cfm?ID=745 (accessed on December 7, 2011). The Indian populace is not related to the local Sri Lankan Tamils even though there are a few historic overlaps. Today, the two Tamil-speaking groups maintain their own, separate identities.

[5]This term is usually referred to the elites who came out of the University of Oxford and University of Cambridge.

of Trincomalee harbour, from where the Royal Navy had operated during the Second World War. Even thereafter, Ceylon continued to be a Dominion of the British Empire until it declared itself a Republic on May 22, 1972, renaming itself Sri Lanka. Subsequently, a Second Republican Constitution came into force in 1978, based on the French model.

Meanwhile, the evolving domestic political scenario was not without problems. The Ceylon National Congress (CNC), which led the independence movement, was riddled with internal sectarian differences along caste and language lines. Linguistic identity became the major fault line, adding to the complexities of an already vexed minority-majority politics. In 1939, the country witnessed a major Sinhala-Tamil riot, followed by relatively peaceful years until 1956. It was that year when the ethnic issue was once again triggered by the introduction of the Official Language Act by Prime Minister SWRD Bandaranaike. This was dubbed the 'Sinhala Only' Act. The Tamil language was rendered secondary to Sinhala. Consequently, the Sinhala-speaking population had an advantage over Tamil speakers in government employment opportunities. The Act, thus, affected a large proportion of the current bureaucracy, who were Tamils. By the late 1960s and early 1970s, the government machinery was predominantly staffed by Sinhalese. This Act, fuelled by 'affirmative action policy' and the 'policy of standardisation,' became a catalyst to inciting Tamil militancy and secessionist movements on the island. Although the Act was diluted in 1958, the damage had already been done. In any case, the Act's core aspects, those most responsible for alienating Tamils, were not changed.[6]

[6]The Tamil Language (Special Provisions) Act was introduced on September 3, 1958 as a means to reduce the impact of the 'Sinhala Only' Act. This new provision provided for the use of Tamil language as a medium of instruction, as a medium of examination for admission to the Public Service, for use in state correspondence and for administrative purposes in the Northern and Eastern provinces. For details, see P. A. Ghosh, *Ethnic Conflict in Sri Lanka and Role of Indian Peace Keeping Force (IPKF)* (APH Publishing, 1999).

POST-INDEPENDENCE INSURGENCIES

While contemporary Sri Lankan history is clouded by the Tamil issue, the nation faced its first domestic insurrection from left-wing Janatha Vimukthi Peramuna (JVP) militants in the 1970s. The JVP rebellion was essentially limited to southern Sinhala regions. The resulting government crackdown was violent, with a number of young JVP cadres losing their lives. However, with the government crackdown and rising Tamil militancy, the JVP would transform itself from an organisation of the oppressed and marginalised to a conservative Sinhala political party.

The Tamil issue took on a militant form beginning in the 1970s and would continue for three decades. While several government initiatives sought to appease the Tamils, they were found wanting. Of these efforts, the hopeful Bandaranaike-Chelvanayakam Pact of 1957, for example, failed to meet Tamil aspirations. After the 1975 assassination of Jaffna's Mayor, Alfred Duraiyappah, political violence became an integral aspect of the Tamil question in northern parts of Sri Lanka. In 1983, the anti-Tamil riots became a watershed event in recent Sri Lankan history. Post-riots, a mass exodus of the Tamil population led to hardening stances as political opposition became armed insurgency. After 1983, the Tamil issue became synonymous with militancy and (eventually) terrorism, with a number of Tamil groups supporting the cause of an independent 'Tamil Eelam.' Of the then prevalent militant organisations, the LTTE became the only group able to sustain its struggle into the new millennium.

Efforts to find a political solution to the Tamil question proved futile even after Indian intervention between 1987 and 1990. India's involvement in finding a political solution to the ethnic issue was the result of the 1987 Indo-Sri Lankan Accord and Operation Poomalai before that. During Operation Poomalai, the Indian Air Force air-dropped essential supplies to the besieged city of Jaffna. The operation reflected India's concern to find a peaceful solution to ethnic issues in Sri Lanka. The Indo-Sri Lanka Agreement resulted in the 13th Amendment to the Sri Lankan Constitution, which officially recognised Tamil as a national language along with Sinhala. The amendment also established increased federalism in the form of more autonomous provincial councils.

In order to enforce a ceasefire agreement and disarm Tamil militants, an Indian Peace Keeping Force (IPKF) was sent to Sri Lanka in 1987. While most Tamil groups entered into an accommodation with Sri Lankan government on the IPKF, the LTTE resented India's military presence. Hostilities between the two groups soon escalated into violence. The IPKF lost some 1,200 personnel,[7] while LTTE suffered a much higher casualty rate.

After the IPKF and failure of the Indo-Sri Lanka Agreement, India withdrew from Sri Lanka. Soon after in 1991, Rajiv Gandhi, architect of the Indo-Sri Lanka Agreement, was assassinated by an LTTE suicide bomber. The subsequent revival of hostilities and Tamil Tiger violence included conventional warfare, guerrilla warfare and bombings across the island. Repeated governmental efforts—involving both peacemaking initiatives and military offensives—were in vain. The only possible exception was the recapturing of Jaffna in 1995-96.

A final bid for a peaceful resolution was sponsored by Norway in 2002. The effort resulted in the decommissioning of weapons, the reopening of the road between Jaffna and rest of Sri Lanka, and engaging in several rounds of peace talks between government and LTTE. However, these failed to find a lasting solution to Sri Lanka's ethnic problem. The LTTE used peace talks as a pretext to gain more time for weapons procurement and recruitment. Meanwhile, the 9/11 terror attacks were a major blow to the LTTE. The group was branded as a 'foreign terrorist organisation.'

[7]R.K. Radhakrishnan, "Kalam pays tributes at IPKF memorial," *The Hindu*, January 22, 2012, available at http://www.thehindu.com/news/international/article2823050.ece (accessed on February 01, 2012).

Consequently, their funding and arms procurement activities were adversely affected.

Meanwhile, the 2005 presidential elections brought Mahinda Rajapaksa to the helm of government, and he initiated military operations against the LTTE with a greater degree of coordination and intelligence inputs. The single-minded focus of the Rajapaksa government to find a military solution to the Tamil problem resulted in a decisive blow to the LTTE. The supremo, Vellupillai Prabhakaran, was killed in May 2009. However, the LTTE defeat cannot be equated with a final solution to the Tamil problem. Issues may resurface if the government is unable to find a lasting political solution that ensures a Tamil return to the Sri Lankan mainstream.

INDIA-SRI LANKA RELATIONS

The quality of India-Sri Lanka relations has vacillated. During the independence era, leaders of India's freedom movement—such as Mahatma Gandhi and Jawaharlal Nehru—toured Ceylon extensively, becoming icons for Tamil youth. However, problems first arose between New Delhi and Colombo when post-Independence Ceylon passed hasty laws rendering stateless and disenfranchised over a million Upcountry Tamils of recent Indian origin (India Origin Tamils (IOTs) or Plantation Tamils).

A number of factors caused the elite Sinhala rulers to feel uncomfortable, including the left-leaning political identity of the Upcountry Tamil labour class. The growth in numbers of Upcountry Tamils made realistic the possibility that future generations would compete with Sri Lankan Tamils for government jobs that had, to that point, been their near exclusive domain. Except for Ceylon Tamil Congress leader SJV Chelvanayagam, who founded the Federal Party (also known as the 'Tamil Aarasu Kadchi' or Tamil Rulers' Party) in the heretofore politically inactive East, the Sri Lankan Tamil community was in accordance with the Sinhala-majority government marginalising and expelling the Upcountry Tamils.

Fresh off partition-induced problems and nascent nation-building, India did precious little in the first post-independence decade to assuage the hurt and loss of the Upcountry Tamils, who had traditionally been left with little pride or possession. Meanwhile, Indian Prime Minister Jawaharalal Nehru's reported statement that Indian expatriates should treat adopted nations as their own did little to ease the situation, which was true both for Upcountry Tamils or the Sri Lankan Tamils after the 'Sinhala Only' law. Additionally, the fledgling Dravida Munnetra Kazhagam (DMK), founded in 1949, was too new to greatly impact the situation.

Although India signed the Sirimavo-Shastri Pact of 1964 and the Sirivamo-Indira Pact of 1966, embracing the neglected Indian Tamils of Sri Lanka, Prime Minister Nehru had also signed a 1950s-era agreement with his Ceylonese counterpart to address the issue. The agreements provided for the safety and security of the Upcountry Tamils in Ceylon. India later agreed to take a substantial portion of the Tamil labour from the Sri Lankan estates back to India. The advent of the ethnic war and consequent secession of ferry services between the two countries contributed to Colombo's accepting all those left behind as Sri Lankan citizens. Another law was then passed to accept Upcountry Tamil refugees in Indian camps and their future progeny as Sri Lankan citizens.

India's engagement with the Sri Lankan Tamil community was based on the misguided premise that Chennai understood them better. Indian policymakers and planners did not fully comprehend local dynamics in Ceylon and suggested remedies to Sri Lanka's ethnic ills that had little legitimate basis (they were focused on good governance rather than constituency-based solutions).

India had a Cold War-era anxiety focused on keeping America from unduly influencing its island-neighbour. India was uncomfortable when Washington negotiated with Colombo for the war vintage oil tank farm in Trincomalee and a Voice of America (VoA) transmitting station.[8] However, India did very little to ease the Sri Lankan state's suspicion which were rooted in the 1971 Bangladesh war and India's support for the "Mukhti Bhahini" guerrillas in erstwhile East Pakistan. In other words, Colombo's anxiety about India soft-pedalling the Tamil aspirations in Sri Lanka was not handled appropriately by New Delhi. If anything, the (now acknowledged) Indian aid, assistance, training, and weapons for Tamil militant groups—assistance that took place for over a decade before New Delhi officially entered the scene—was a recipe for disaster which none seemed to realise.

Meanwhile, the June-July 1987 Operation Poomalai (a humanitarian initiative to air-drop food and medicines for the besieged Tamil population in the north at Vadamarachchi) and consequent India-Sri Lanka Agreement signalled that the Sri Lankan State and Sinhala polity viewed India as an unwelcomed 'big brother.' Furthermore, the commitment of political support, if not outright loyalty, from Tamils in India further infuriated the Sri Lankan leadership. The IPKF years not only saw Tamil moderates running down the Accord that they previously had India negotiate and sign but also witnessed the LTTE working with Sri Lanka's government and armed forces to remove the IPKF. The 1991 assassination of then Indian Prime Minister Rajiv Gandhi by an LTTE suicide-bomber in Tamil Nadu and the humiliating, untimely withdrawal of the IPKF meant that India's Sri Lanka policy would be linked to Prabhakaran's death.

By 2000, India recognised the need to proactively engage its neighbours and regional powers in order to attain major power-

[8]Bureau of South and Central Asian Affaires, U.S. State Department, "Background Note: Sri Lanka," available online at http://www.state.gov/r/pa/ei/bgn/5249.htm (accessed on December 21, 2011).

status in Asia (and beyond). India's strengthened engagement with Sri Lanka was marked by the arrival of Norway as peacemaker between the Sri Lankan government and the LTTE. The involvement of an external power in the internal conflict in Sri Lanka convinced Indian policymakers to strengthen its own engagement with Colombo. The post-9/11 global situation compelled the LTTE to tone down its actions and prompted the group to sign a ceasefire agreement with the government. However, the failure of Government-LTTE talks, under Norwegian facilitation,[9] eventually led to Eelam War IV, when well-prepared government forces under determined political leadership vanquished the LTTE.

President Rajapaksa came into office with the determination to launch a "fight-to-finish" campaign against the LTTE. However, within the Indian and Sri Lankan establishments, this was seen as a farfetched objective. Analysts believe that the three-year period within which the Rajapaksa government wiped out the LTTE would not have been possible without Indian support. Sri Lankan leadership–President Rajapaksa, Defence Secretary Gotabaya Rajapaksa, Economic Development Minister Basil Rajapaksa (both the President's brothers), and President's Secretary Lalith Weeratunga–have all acknowledged this fact. The ethnic war's conclusion and LTTE exit helped bridge the trust gap between India and Sri Lanka to an extent.

What is often misunderstood is the importance of the 'China' factor to New Delhi's new approach to Colombo. While New Delhi also stands ready to help the Sri Lankan Tamils, India acknowledges that it must work with and through Sri Lankan state institutions and political establishment. The polity in Tamil Nadu is unwilling to recognise this recent dynamic, partly because of inadequate understanding. While narrowing the trust gap

[9]"Sri Lanka ends Norway peace role," *al- Jazeera*, April 14, 2009, available online at http://www.aljazeera.com/news/europe/2009/04/200941435155729581.html (accessed on January 13, 2012).

between India and Sri Lanka remains difficult, especially given India's vote in Geneva, New Delhi needs to craft a policy that does not jeopardise the bilateral relationship. Only such a nuanced policy will ensure a satisfactory solution to both the Tamil question and balancing China's increased influence in Sri Lanka.

However, several elements have boosted India-Sri Lanka bilateral relations in recent years, and they must be further strengthened. Last-minute Sri Lankan reservations to the signing of a Comprehensive Economic Partnership Agreement (CEPA) with India notwithstanding (it is four years since CEPA[10] was put on hold), trade relations have improved under the Free Trade Agreement (FTA) regime. This was the first FTA India signed with any country and has become a model for future agreements. Tourism has also thrived. Indians top the list of foreign tourists visiting Sri Lanka, and tourism is one of the largest contributors to Sri Lanka's forex reserves. Cultural exchanges at the people-to-people level have also revived in the post-war era, with more Sinhalese travelling to India on pilgrimage visits to Buddhist centres. Tamils, including Upcountry Tamils from Sri Lanka, continued visiting Tamil Nadu even during the war years, and this remains unchanged.

There is an acknowledgment in Sri Lanka that the country must learn from and participate in the Indian economic growth story. There needs to be an even greater realisation in New Delhi that economic interdependence with its neighbours will be a key factor in defining bilateral relations and bettering economic outcomes for both partners. In this context, it remains crucial to ensure that domestic political considerations in India (principally those deriving from Tamil Nadu) do not jeopardise continued and future progress on this front.

[10]Ministry of Commerce, Government of India, "Agreement on South Asia Free Trade Area (SAFTA)," available online at http://commerce.nic.in/india_rta.htm (accessed on March 14, 2012).

II

Geopolitics and Strategic Aspects

Sri Lanka's importance for India and other countries stems from its strategic location in the Indian Ocean. It is both a gateway to East Asia and a doorstep to South Asia for the rest of the world. Its large number of natural ports and harbours makes Sri Lanka attractive from both commercial and military perspectives. Sri Lanka's current political leadership is keen on developing the country as an essential crossroads for international trade. In his vision document titled *Mahinda Chintana*, President Rajapaksa stated that he is "determined to make our country [Sri Lanka] the centre of the Asian silk route once again taking advantage of its unique geographical location."

Sri Lanka is home to the world's second largest natural harbour—Trincomalee. The entrance to the harbour is four miles wide and five miles across, east to west. The inner harbour (which lies in the north) covers about 12 square miles and is securely enclosed by outcrops of huge rocks and small islets. The harbour was an important reconnaissance and control hub for the British during the Second World War. Since then, the U.S. has sought to lease Trincomalee as a refuelling and recreation facility for its Seventh Fleet based in Diego Garcia and also as a NATO bridgehead. Strategically located near the Bay of Bengal, Trincomalee is often described as one of Sri Lanka's "most valuable assets." The harbour also provides natural conditions for strategic nuclear submarine bases.[11] This raises concerns for India's strategists, given China's interests in the area. Adding on to these concerns is China's interest in the Hambantota Port. With a capacity to berth 33 vessels at any given time, Hambantota is the largest harbour in South Asia. At least 20 per cent of the shipping traffic, mainly oil tankers, call at this port, saving nearly three days' sailing time. These obvious commercial and strategic advantages of Sri Lanka have drawn China to invest in the development of not only the Hambantota Port but also the Colombo Port.

The development of Hambantota Port by China,[12] which commenced on January 15, 2008 by the China Harbour Engineering Company and Sinohydro Corporation, is seen as a "pearl" in the 'Chinese String of Pearls' policy aimed at containing India. This policy, in turn, has prompted India to undertake active counter-measures. India has been trying to cast its net wide and reach well beyond the region. It is actively pursuing a multi-pronged response strategy seeking to neutralise Chinese influence in its immediate neighbourhood by simultaneously courting states on China's periphery and beyond, many of whom are apprehensive of China's growing assertiveness.

[11]Ramesh Somasundaram, "Strategic Significance of Sri Lanka," quoted in P.K. Balachandran, "Sri Lanka's Strategic Importance," *The Hindustan Times,* June 01, 2006, available at http://www.island.lk/2005/06/01/features1.html.

[12]Construction of this port commenced on January 15, 2008 by the China Harbour Engineering Company and Sinohydro Corporation. The cost of the first phase was $360 million and $76.5 million for the bunker terminal. As much as 85 per cent of the funding is provided by the Chinese government and the remaining 15 per cent is provided by the Sri Lanka Ports Authority. The first phase completed five months ahead of schedule and became operational in November 2010. The planned second phase will include a container terminal and is expected to be completed by 2014. The second stage of the port is estimated to cost around U.S. $750 million. The third phase will include a dockyard. Upon completion, the port will cover 4,000 acres (16 km^2) of land and accommodate 33 vessels at any given time, making it the largest port in South Asia.

Figure 1: Hambantota Port Plan 5

Source: The Asian Tribune, November 1, 2007.

In an attempt to balance the equation, Colombo has allowed India to open a consulate in Hambantota as well as in Jaffna. But the US $450 million agreement, signed in September 2010 with the China Merchants Holdings for the development of Colombo Port, has clearly underlined the challenge India is likely to face from China in the region.

The increased involvement of China in Sri Lanka, among other countries in South Asia is likely to alter the traditional understanding between India and Sri Lanka over the role of external players. For instance, it will be a daunting task for India to enforce some of the points of the India-Sri Lanka Accord of July 1987, wherein both countries had agreed that:

(1) Trincomalee or any other port of Sri Lanka will not be made available for military use by any country in a manner prejudicial to India's interests.

(2) The work of restoring and operating the Trincomalee oil tank farm will be undertaken as a joint venture between India and Sri Lanka.

(3) Sri Lanka's agreement with foreign broadcasting organisations will be reviewed to ensure that any facilities set

up are used solely as public broadcasting facilities and not for any military or intelligence purposes.[13]

The worst case scenario for an Indian strategist would involve the lurking (and basing) of Chinese submarines in its immediate neighbourhood. Indian strategic thinker RR Ramachandra Rao stated in 1954 that India had "very real interest in ensuring that no hostile power should establish itself in Ceylon. Ceylon is within Indian defence area, at the very heart centre of the Indian Ocean and India was worried about the influx of foreign intelligence personnel into Sri Lanka defence."[14]

Figure 2: President Rajapaksa's Vision for Sri Lanka

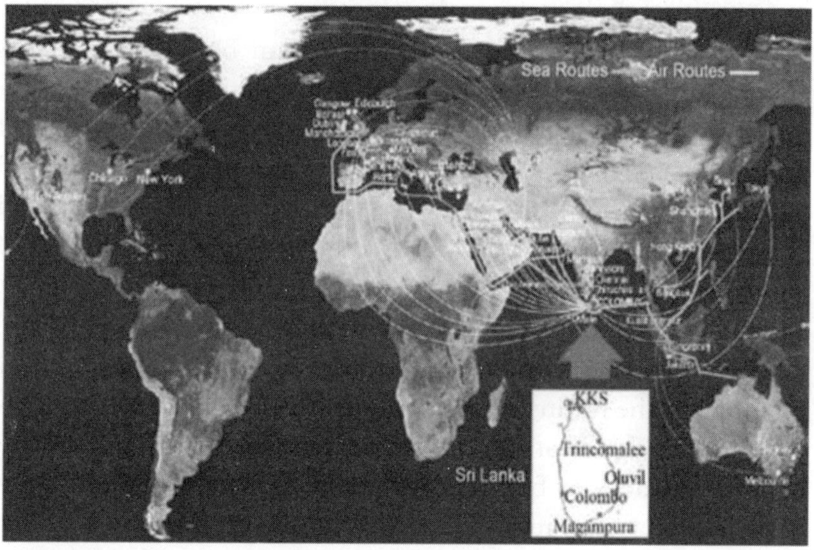

Source: Mahinda Chintana 2010: Vision for the Future, Department of National Planning, Ministry of Finance and Planning, Government of Sri Lanka.

[13]The text of the agreement and the exchange of letters available at http://www.satp.org/satporgtp/countries/shrilanka/document/papers/indo_srilanka_agreement.htm.

[14]Cited in P.K. Balachandran, "Sri Lanka's Strategic Importance," Lanka Newspapers, May 31, 2005, available at http://www.lankanewspapers.com/news/2005/5/2266.html.

MARITIME SECURITY AND RESOURCE DYNAMICS

A major factor for Sri Lanka's strategic importance is its location in the Indian Ocean. Rising economic globalisation has enhanced the importance of seaborne trade manifold, with 70 per cent of global oil trade and 50 per cent of container traffic passing through the Indian Ocean and its various choke points. About 70 per cent of India's trade passes through this region. In addition, 80 per cent of China's oil and 90 per cent of its trade is carried out via the Indian Ocean. It is estimated that 36,000 ships pass through the Hambantota Port annually, including 4,500 oil tankers. Interestingly, the seas near Dondra Head in southern Sri Lanka form a virtual choke point in the region.

The Hambantota Port is also important because it oversees energy supply lines to the "demand periphery" of energy-dependent nations like India, China, and Japan. India's own oil import dependence, at current levels of consumption, is expected to rise to 91.6 per cent by 2020. This has led to an enhanced sensitivity to the security of the SLOCs (Sea Lines of Communication) and the choke points of the region. Naturally, SLOCs form the lifelines for these countries.

Given the huge volume of traffic, which is likely to grow manifold in the future, the vulnerability factor of these waterways will increase significantly. The vulnerabilities could be in the form of piracy attacks or blockade of certain ports. Protection of the SLOCs along this region becomes a major imperative and a potential area for collaboration between major Asian players. So far this has been limited; the collaboration has been between major powers and littoral states.

The threat to maritime security also comes principally from transnational crime syndicates operating from Southeast Asia to Europe and beyond, using the sea lines for human trafficking and smuggling of drugs and weapons. Sri Lanka's role in ensuring maritime security in the region is likely to be critical.

In addition to its geographical positioning, Sri Lanka presents a resource matrix that increases its importance in the global economy. Sri Lanka's natural resources, both explored and unexplored, add to its advantage. It is rich in natural resources: tea, rubber, spices, and mineral resources such as graphite, gems (including sapphires), limestone, mineral sands, copper, iron, iron ore, dolomite, calcite, shale, clay, kaolin, and more significantly phosphates and hydropower among others. Additionally, there has been discovery of some of the largest oil and gas fields in South Asia. The recent discovery of gas fields in the Mannar area straddling the maritime boundary with India is a case in point. There are also oil and gas reserves that it shares with India, found in the Cauveri basin located in the north. Many countries have shown interest in carrying out explorations, from Russia's Gazprom to Vietnam's PVEP (PetroVietnam Exploration Production Corp), to France's Total and some Australian, U.S., and European companies.[15] The discovery of energy (oil) in and around the Sri Lankan waters could profoundly transform the great game being played in the region and enhance its strategic leverages, making it a strategic driver.

However, there are likely to be sensitivities and counter-sensitivities on the presence of certain "extra-regional" powers. Strategists say that this could turn out to be the South China Sea in reverse for Sino-Indian ties. New Delhi has disregarded Beijing's protests and asserted its determination to collaborate with Vietnam to explore for oil in the disputed waters of the South China Sea. Now it may well become "payback time" when China decides whether or not to accept Colombo's fervent invitation to prospect for oil in the Palk Strait in the waters that are near India's southern coastline.

Thus, New Delhi is frantically lobbying mandarins in Colombo not to disregard Indian sensitivities by allowing the

[15]M.K. Bhadrakumar, "Sri Lankan Ghosts Haunt India," *Asia Times Online*, March 15, 2012, available at http://www.atimes.com/atimes/South_Asia/NC15Df05.html (accessed on March 15, 2012).

Chinese to come in such close proximity to its coastline. A team from India's oil giant ONGC Videsh Limited (OVL) visited Colombo and made a counter-offer, which was followed by an extended four-day visit by then External Affairs Minister SM Krishna. Sri Lanka remained noncommittal. A senior official of the Petroleum Ministry in Colombo told the British Broadcasting Corporation (BBC):

> They [Indians] have a lot of experience. Their knowledge is more than ours—they have a lot of seismic knowledge. And they have the funding—if we're picking partners, they tick the boxes. But we'd like to see a diversity of investors.[16]

The official also said Colombo would "write to the whole world," including China.[17] Sri Lanka's decision to go with any of the international firms will have significant implications for the Indian security calculus, especially if the firm happens to be a Chinese one.

Sri Lanka is also ideal for establishing itself as the next international telecommunications exchange hub, with which it can pitch for a premier position as the next knowledge economy hub. According to the World Bank, Sri Lanka has the best telecommunications technology in South Asia and the best tariff rates as well. Being an island, it is well placed to receive all submarine cables. The Sri Lanka Telecommunication Regulatory Commission is planning to lay an extensive fibre optic network that will cover the entire island and connect all households, allowing access to broadband and other high-speed communication

[16]Charles Haviland, "Sri Lanka's potential oil reserves spark global interest," *BBC News*, March 12, 2012, available at http://www.bbc.co.uk/news/business-17337054.

[17]Charles Haviland, "Sri Lanka's potential oil reserves spark global interest," *BBC News*, March 12, 2012, available at http://www.bbc.co.uk/news/business-17337054.

services. This aspect has again been explored by the Chinese telecommunication giants like Huawei, who have seized upon the idea and the opportunity. Thus, despite its small size, Sri Lanka has the potential to wield considerable strategic muscle.

THE INDIAN OCEAN RIVALRY

The Indian Ocean Region (IOR) is increasingly being characterised by strategic competition and rivalry, both from external actors and littoral states. The predominant concern today has to do with China's increasing presence in the region and, to a lesser extent, that of the U.S.

China's interests are not only to enter Sri Lanka in a big way, but also to build regional interconnectivity in order to make Chinese goods more competitive. This is particularly seen beneficial for China-Africa trade. For instance, the operationalisation of the new deep-sea port in 2015, currently under construction by China at Kyaukphyu on Myanmar's western coast, and the construction of a

Figure 3: China's Planned Route for Greater Interconnectivity

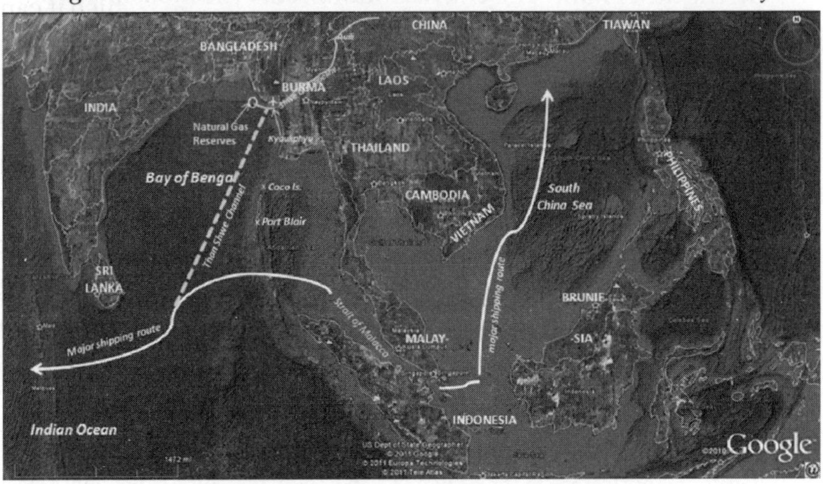

Source: Arakan Indobhasa Blog, available at http://arakanindobhasaa.blogspot.in/2011/11/massive-military-built-up-at-ann-arakan.html

railway line connecting the port with the Kunming region in southern China, will be a major boost for China's trade. On the other hand, Hambantota—the Sri Lankan port built with Chinese assistance—is strategically located south of Sri Lanka and has the potential to compete with Singapore. The interconnectivity that China achieves through linking Hambantota with Kyaukphyu in Myanmar will offer benefits to Beijing, both in economic and strategic terms. For one, the new route will reduce the distance and the resulting costs. Meanwhile, it is strategically important for China to reduce its dependence on the Malacca Straits. China's development of the Hambantota port is also a strategic concern for India. China could potentially set up listening posts and signals intelligence stations that could be activated in times of conflict.

China has continued to argue that its presence in the IOR is determined by commercial interests and ensuring protection of the SLOCs. This argument is only part of China's ambitions in the region.[17a] Beijing's growing assertive behaviour along with unresolved territorial disputes, including maritime ones, have added to the threat perception in New Delhi about China.

On the other hand, the U.S. is undoubtedly the most important player in the IOR with its capacity for military power projection and a dedicated strategy to continue with its preeminent position. At present, the U.S. has deployed three carrier groups—USS John C. Stennis, USS Carl Vinson, and USS Abraham Lincoln—in the vicinity of the Persian Gulf. The U.S. military facility in the Indian Ocean is based in Diego Garcia which was established as a base—Naval Support Facility Diego Garcia or Permanent Joint

[17a]In its first Blue Book on Indian Ocean Region, China clearly spells out its strategy moving beyond economic interests. It says, "China's diplomatic strategy in the past has been based on the traditional concept of moderation, and striven to maintain the status quo. With changes in the relations among countries in the IOR and in the international situation, China's diplomacy should also change. A clear development strategy in the Indian Ocean Region for China is not only a sign of China's self-confidence, and also a clear demonstration of China's strategic interests in the Indian Ocean Region." See Ananth Krishnan, "China Details Indian Ocean Strategy and Interests," *The Hindu,* June 9, 2013.

Operational Base. The primary operational responsibility of this naval facility is to provide logistics support to the U.S. forces deployed in the Indian Ocean and in the Persian Gulf. Media reports suggest that the U.S. navy is planning to upgrade this facility to a submarine base, which can facilitate the berthing of SSGN nuclear submarines.

U.S. Fifth Fleet (C5F), an Echelon III command, supports all naval operations in the U.S. Central Command (CENTCOM) area of responsibility (AOR), including parts of the Indian Ocean. It encompasses about 7.5 million square miles and includes the Arabian Gulf, Red Sea, Gulf of Oman, and parts of the Indian Ocean. This expanse, comprising 25 countries, includes Bahrain, Saudi Arabia, United Arab Emirates (UAE), Iran, Iraq, Pakistan, and Somalia. The Fifth Fleet is the full equivalent of the Sixth and Seventh Fleets. It typically comprises a CVBG (carrier battle group comprising an aircraft carrier and four principal surface combatants, two nuclear-powered submarines, and a support ship), an ARG, and the MEF (comprising the surface ships of Destroyer Squadron 50 of the Pacific Fleet). In addition, submarines, maritime patrol and reconnaissance aircraft, support ships, and afloat prepositioning ships also operate routinely in the Arabian Sea and the Indian Ocean. On average, the Commander, Fifth Fleet, has some 15-35 major warships under his operational command at any given time. The Fifth Fleet on average has at least one Aircraft Carrier Battle Group and an Amphibious Ready Group among other naval assets.

Despite its military presence, the U.S. has remained preoccupied in Afghanistan and Iraq for a decade and the strategic vacuum has been tactically filled in by China, posing itself as a rival to America's interests in the region. India, on the other hand, is not only nervous about its own ability to balance China but is also concerned about America's ability, intention and willingness to contain China, particularly in the economic domain.

India's concerns in this regard are very similar to those of Japan: is India or Japan worth the cost for the U.S. to antagonise

China in the IOR? New Delhi has accordingly begun to stress the importance of engaging with the region in the economic, political, and military arena. The Indian Ocean Naval Symposium (IONS) initiated under India's leadership was a step in this regard to forge closer ties with the regional navies. Just as China has adopted the "Far-Sea" defence strategy, pursuing its economic and energy interests, the Indian leadership, both political and naval, is also convinced that maritime security dimensions will have an increasingly important role in managing the new dynamics. While the regional architecture today is essentially shaped by the U.S., China, India, and Japan to an extent, the geographic and geo-economic contours of Sri Lanka will give it a determining role in redefining the Asia-Pacific architecture.

Given these developments, Sri Lanka could emerge as a major trading hub or a Dubai of South Asia in the years ahead. Sri Lanka's plans to develop new ports and hubs will likely enhance the role for Colombo in the near future. These plans are likely to be materialised with significant help from China for two reasons: one, even if the Sri Lankan leadership were to approach India, New Delhi does not have the financial wherewithal to offer such assistance to Colombo; and two, China has both the financial and infrastructural capacity—along with strategic interest—to do so. While no country including Sri Lanka would like to completely depend on China for their growth—and in fact would like to involve India to balance Chinese dominance in port and allied infrastructure developments—they are not in a position to reject China's assistance, which is considered critical for their economic development. This is particularly the case when India's commitment has not been forthcoming.

Meanwhile, the global shipping industry has been in doldrums since 2008; an indicator of this is the Baltic Dry Index (BDI). It was above 12,000 points and is presently at 700 (although it was between 2,000-3,000 in 2010 largely as a result of quantitative easing). The reasons for this predicament are several, particularly imbalance in supply and demand of shipping services, as well as higher fuel costs. As a result, it can be argued that this industry is unlikely to recover in the near future and there could be further concentration within the industry resulting in creation of oligopolies and dominance of markets. In fact, as a strategy for survival, shipping companies are forming alliances, reducing speeds, and increasing the size of ships.

All these strategies will hurt India's trade in a variety of ways. India's ports are inefficient in varying degrees due to reasons such as labour productivity, poor connectivity, capacity restraints, limited draft, and lack of funds. As such, they will not be able to handle large vessels efficiently. Smaller vessels, on the other hand, indicate loss of scale economies, transhipments and higher costs for Indian exim cargoes leading to eventual loss of competitive advantage vis-à-vis China. This has further implications for Indian industries, employment, and revenue collection, among others.

India has no option but to proactively play the game if it seeks to have a role in the emerging Indian Ocean dynamics. India has been requested to participate in the Dawei Port in Myanmar and rail network in Sri Lanka and Myanmar. So as not to lose the edge, the Government of India should at the earliest make a commitment to South and Southeast Asian countries in order to stay relevant in this game.

SRI LANKA'S PLANS

Sri Lanka's own ambitions are expanding. It imagines itself as taking on a new role in the emerging regional dynamics, as a commercial and energy hub of South Asia. *Mahinda Chintana,* in fact, identifies the establishment of an economic zone in the areas between Hambantota and Embilipitiya, essentially for internal supplies while also offering services to foreign ships. The document also identifies undertaking a programme to provide foreign employment in the commercial-naval fields. The importance of the region is also highlighted by the fact that Colombo plans to set up a naval training school in Hambantota. All of these programmes are indicative of the strategic importance of Hambantota in Sri Lanka's geostrategic calculations.

Sri Lanka could adopt the Rotterdam model to become a major commercial and transit centre for goods from Europe, Latin America, and Africa to Asia and Australia. This could open up various possibilities. On the one hand, there could be further strengthening of collaboration among countries such as the U.S., India, Japan, and Australia as an effort to manage China. On the other hand, given the huge Chinese investments in several of Sri Lanka's infrastructure projects as also Beijing's critical political support (from the days of the LTTE war), it could be that Colombo steers towards Beijing.

A third possibility is that Sri Lanka becomes an international financing centre like London. This could again work in two ways: Sri Lanka either integrates with the Western international financing centres or become a Yuan surrogate. In either scenario, while Sri Lanka may have enough elbow room to bargain a better deal, it could also become the strategic battleground, forcing it to make tough choices.

NAVAL AMBITIONS

Sri Lanka's primary concerns were internal and not external. Therefore, its maritime capabilities were confined to combat sea-based asymmetric warfare. The Sri Lankan Navy as an institution has proven capability and expertise for combating sea-based asymmetric warfare, but the same cannot be said about its deep-sea assets. The nation's naval assets are largely focused on offshore patrolling crafts, littoral attack crafts, amphibious warfare vessels, and other relatively smaller vessels. The rationale for this kind of a force structure was the navy's role in overcoming the challenge posed by the LTTE (Sea Tigers) with their expertise to skilfully carry out sea-based guerrilla warfare. It was also to assist the land forces in discharging their combat duties.

In recent times, Sri Lanka has expressed unspecified plans for a "blue water"–capable navy which would complement its strategic location in the Indian Ocean. Sri Lanka wants to attain this "blue water" capability with help from "regional friendly countries." However, its capacity and resources aimed at such a dramatic transformation are in serious doubt. Though they have raised an able Coast Guard for carrying out constabulary functions, there has not been any significant change till date in the type of vessels possessed by the Sri Lankan Navy. Most of the warships are small vessels that are suited for littoral and coastal security. Sri Lanka is also working towards a maritime security arrangement with Maldives and India, the negotiations on which are in their nascent stages and proceeding smoothly.

Looking at future possibilities, the Hambantota port will potentially have military use and can be converted into a naval base if required. The port developed by China can also be used for refuelling and bunkering facilities. However, China's military capability to protect its military assets in the IOR by 2025 is likely to remain inadequate and the geographical distance from the mainland will only magnify China's vulnerability. In the foreseeable future, Beijing will likely be preoccupied with developments in its immediate neighbourhood, particularly the South China Sea and East China Sea disputes. Its military is likely to remain focussed on addressing the growing challenges emanating from the waters closer to home.

The Chinese actions in the region have largely been reactionary. There is a remote possibility that U.S. dependence on the SLOCs passing through IOR might lessen in the near future. In such a scenario, the U.S. will be more inclined to reduce its overwhelming role in protecting the SLOCs, thus creating a vacuum which China might like to fill, given its dependence on these SLOCs. To avoid such a situation, India should work towards building a security framework with other like-minded nations. This calls for a deeper engagement with immediate neighbours such as Maldives and Sri Lanka for creating such architecture. This should be complemented by a more expansive framework comprising Australia and Japan, both with considerable interest and capacity in the security of the SLOCs in the region.

On the economic front, China will continue to be a rival. India can balance this by collaborating with the West in crafting a deeper and more broad-based economic engagement with Sri Lanka. India's measures to strengthen regional connectivity and collaboration in South and Southeast Asia will increase New Delhi's options in the region.

BALANCING ACT

It is clear that Sri Lanka occupies a niche geostrategic position in the IOR, making it attractive to most powers with stakes in the region. Take for instance, the case of China. China, which is an active player in IOR, looks at Sri Lanka as a long-term strategic investment with an eye on the future. The decision, at one level, is driven by the compulsions of protecting the seaborne trade of China and lifeline energy routes; at another level, it is about engaging the neighbours of India to checkmate New Delhi on the classic principle of "engage the neighbour of your prospective competitor."

The strategic power-play that has been ongoing for decades now appears to be intensifying, particularly with both India and China trying to woo the Indian Ocean littoral states with investments and concessional loans for development. Sri Lanka has gained from this power rivalry both during the war as well as in the post-war period. It is not a secret that Sri Lanka has repeatedly used the China card in India and has had no reservations, either, about using the India card in China and Pakistan to obtain whatever it wanted in furthering its national interests. Sri Lanka has obtained military assistance from China, India, Pakistan, Iran, Israel, South Africa, and other western countries including the U.S.

However, India has been considerably constrained by its internal politics in developing far deeper relations, including military—an aspect that needs to be overcome by either covert or overt means since, after all, Sri Lanka holds an important key to India's security. India should not let the China factor dominate its relationship with Sri Lanka. Building a naval base in Sri Lanka could become a strategic overreach for Beijing. While India should bear in mind the strategic cost of Sri Lanka, it need not go overboard in offering the proverbial carrots to Sri Lanka.

III

The Political and Military Landscape

The Political Landscape

Sri Lanka's political landscape, like that of its counterparts in the rest of the Indian subcontinent, reflects a case of caste- and class-based politics. Most of Sri Lanka's dominant political players across the spectrum traditionally come from elite sections of society. The political leadership has been, more or less, dynastic in nature as is the case in the rest of the Indian subcontinent.

To this end, the militancy from the 1970s, first in form of the left-leaning Sinhala Janatha Vimukthi Peramuna (JVP) and later, the Tamil variant of the LTTE, set the ball rolling for a change in the socio-cultural background of the political class. At one level it may not be wrong to suggest that both the JVP and the LTTE movements were supported by the section of population that could not entirely relate to the elite political class in Colombo. It is also an interesting coincidence that both the JVP and the LTTE leadership belonged to the fishing community, the so-called low caste of Sri Lanka. Traditionally, the leadership of mainstream political parties of the Sinhala community and the erstwhile Tamil community were from the upper strata.

The Sri Lankan polity can be broadly divided into a few identifiable groups, namely:

- The Sinhala-based, relatively moderate mainstream political parties represented by the United National Party (UNP) and the Sri Lankan Freedom Party (SLFP).

- The second group comprises what is called 'the Sinhala chauvinistic southern political parties,' such as the JVP and Jathika Hela Urumaya (JHU).
- The third entity is made up of the political parties of Tamil-speaking people: Tamil National Alliance (TNA) of the Sri Lankan Tamils; Sri Lanka Muslim Congress (SLMC) of the Muslims; and the Ceylon Workers Congress (CWC) of the Upcountry or Plantation Tamils of recent Indian origin, referred to as 'Indian Origin Tamils' (IOTs).
- There are other smaller parties in every linguistic and ethnic group whose representation at the national level has been low. Although the Tamil political parties were to unite as a coherent group, first on ethnic basis and then as a linguistic group, they are unable to influence policymaking at the national level. This is primarily due to the inherent divisions in the larger Sinhala polity and society. Additionally, instead of using their political clout to promote the interests of the Tamils, the parties are using ethnicity as a means to achieve their political objectives.

The linguistic identity of Tamils does not reflect in an umbrella political party unlike in the case of the Sinhala linguistic identity. The Tamil-speaking population, to a large extent, can be divided into three groups: the Sri Lankan Tamils dominant in the north and the east; the Muslims concentrated in the east; and the Plantation Tamil who are of Indian origin found in the central highlands. These identities are further categorised by caste equations, rendered even more complicated by their geographic origins.

Furthermore, the Sinhala political spectrum has been stratified into the existing political parties, all representing a section of caste-driven Sri Lankan polity. To this end, the Tamils too are not that far behind. The Tamil militant groups that sprouted in large numbers during the 1980s were a product of the caste divide within the Tamil (Sri Lankan) community. However, the consolidation of the LTTE and its steady rise had, to an extent, brushed aside the caste lines within its ranks. While the LTTE had achieved some success in uniting the Sri Lankan Tamils of both the north and the east, it was not in a position to remove the caste prejudice within the Tamil community.

The post-war Sri Lankan political developments are to be seen in this backdrop. The previous generation of elitist politicians across the board have now been replaced by a new generation of leadership who represent different strata of society, introducing new dynamics in terms of representation of regions, caste, and class in the national political scene. For instance, President Rajapaksa comes from Hambantota, the southernmost part of the country that has a limited presence in mainstream politics, Similarly, Gen. Sarath Fonseka, who won a victory against the LTTE in the final Eelam War, belonged to an intermediate caste outside the traditional power structure.

In the post-LTTE era, the Tamil political dynamics is reflective of caste-based politics that is, in turn, driven by vote-bank interests. While the TNA has emerged as the umbrella political party for the Sri Lankan Tamils, its effectiveness to project itself as a major force is yet to be proved. Whether or not the alliance will stick together in the near future is also subject to speculation. As its name suggests, the alliance comprises of various Tamil political parties and individuals representing different and competing political priorities within a broad-spectrum idea to struggle for greater political power, opportunities and acceptance in post-independent Sri Lanka. The fact is that the TNA in the past was held together by the barrel of the (LTTE) gun and, at present, by Tamil insecurity. This has its own dynamics evident in the uncertainties as well as the inability of Tamils to project themselves as a unified entity.

On the other hand, the Tamil issue has not been synonymous with language but was rather defined by history and geography. Neither the LTTE nor the Tamil political class catered to the needs and aspirations of the Plantation Tamils (Tamils of Indian Origin) or the Muslims. This had resulted in the formation of Muslim and Plantation Tamil political parties independent of the Sri Lankan Tamils, two of the more notable of which are the SLMC and the CWC. Over time, the growing aspirations of these communities and the internal dynamics have resulted in the fracturing of their political clout in electoral terms.

At the same time, Plantation Tamils are also haunted by caste equations, though not to the same extent as the Sri Lankan Tamils. This has resulted in the caste-based Tamil politics within the Plantation Tamil community that is yet to make a significant impact in Sri Lankan politics. On the other hand, the Muslims, despite their monolithically religious and social structure, are now fractured on grounds of economic opportunities brought about by education. Muslim vote-bank politics, like in the case of the Plantation Tamils, is yet to regain a mark at the national level after losing the initial advantage at birth. This is mainly due to internal splits and divisions, for which they have not grown tired of blaming the Sinhala party in power at any given time. However, these developments have already been recognised by the existing mainstream political parties and suitable political accommodation has been worked out, but not always to the advantage of the minorities.

Post-war local body elections are not the appropriate benchmark to analyse the political landscape of Sri Lanka, as the ghost of the civil war was still prevalent at that time. The real test for Sri Lanka's polity will come in the 2015 parliamentary elections and in the 2016 presidential elections or even earlier, if President Rajapaksa decides to call for early polls. These elections could be defining points in the Sri Lankan political evolution since they could (theoretically) help chalk out the nation's political destiny in terms of both the ethnic issue and the electoral system.

The reason for this is that the Sinhala nationalistic political parties like the JVP and the JHU, in the absence of the LTTE, have lost a rallying point. Moreover, the SLFP and the UNP's traditional vote-bank now include the stronghold of the Sinhala-Buddhist nationalist JVP and the JHU. At the same time, the national psyche that was earlier conditioned by the victory over the LTTE would also have already undergone a change. The need for a hardliner or a hawkish leader is likely to diminish and politics is likely to be driven more by economic and development issues.

Thus, Sri Lankan politics is beginning to see new dynamics coming into play with the end of the war against the LTTE. The emerging polity will have to focus on the need for an inclusive political environment, wherein the aspiration of the masses in general and the Tamils in particular would have to be taken into consideration. At present, the Sri Lankan political landscape is dominated by coalition politics, evident even during the presidential polls. As in any other country, coalition politics in Sri Lanka is driven by vote-bank consideration. The coalition partners, in alliance with the larger majority party, are driven by the need to secure and cater to the needs of their respective constituencies. In this background, it would not be long before the Tamil political parties become a part of this political culture, thus adding to the existing political dynamics of the nation.

The existing base and stronghold of the Sinhala political parties, too, could have undergone a change. This could be due to factors such as development and economic issues taking the lead over political ones. It is seen that President Rajapaksa's massive victory in the presidential elections has resulted in the total weakening of the opposition. The opposition in the form of UNP and the rest is unable to field a strong candidate after Fonseka's exit from politics. It can be said that this vacuum within the ranks of the opposition, unless filled in by a credible leader, could result in the scattering of votes for the opposition and also the strengthening of SLFP's monopoly, particularly under the present leadership of President Rajapaksa. However, Rajapaksa could be challenged in the next elections if the government is unable to make a clean start in dealing with ethnic reconciliation, two of the key components of which are the development of the north and the east and finding a political solution to the Tamil problem. The Tamils have to consolidate themselves in order to pose any serious challenge to Rajapaksa in the next elections.

The political settlement of the ethnic issues would be largely decided on two grounds—what is demanded by the Tamil community, and what the government is able to deliver. A political package announced by the government will have to address two issues: the demands of the Tamils for better representation in political, educational institutions and bureaucracy, as well as the government's anxieties on issues such as dealing with the international community on human rights issues and the potential regrouping of Tamil militants in the North and the East. It will be like walking a political tightrope. As of now, the ability of the government to deliver on this front is also determined by the political realities in the Sinhala heartland and on a number of Sinhala-dominant political parties. If the Tamils are able to organise themselves in a more systematic manner and provide the political cushion that the SLFP may need, it may lead to a situation where Rajapaksa's reliance on some of the Sinhala-dominant parties will be reduced. Such a development could ease out the government pressures as it focuses on finding a political solution to the ethnic problem.

FUTURE POLITICAL LANDSCAPE IN SRI LANKA

In order for India to pursue closer relations with Sri Lanka, it is pertinent to look at future potential leaders in the next decade or so. It would do well if India cultivated these leaders even if they are sitting in the opposition today or leaders who might currently be represented in very small numbers. Among the noticeable political leaders in the Sinhala community, apart from President Rajapaksa, are his brother Basil Rajapaksa, his son Namal

Rajapaksa, Prime Minister DM Jayaratna, Irrigation Minister Nimal Siripala de Silva, Higher Education Minister S.B. Dissanayake, Rehabilitation Minister Mahinda Samarasinghe, and Finance Minister Sarath Amunugama. Among the second generation, potential future leaders include: Dilan Perara and Sajjin Was Gunaratna—both from SLFP. From among the bureaucrats, Defence Secretary Gotabaya Rajapaksa (a brother of the president), Treasury Secretary TB Jayasundara and Central Bank Governor Nivad Cabbral, exercise greater clout than their offices command otherwise. Among the UNP leaders, the most prominent are Ranil Wickremesinghe, Sajith Premadasa, Ravi Karunanayake, Party General Secretary Tissa Attanayake, Parliamentary whip John Amaratunga, and veteran leader Karu Jayasuriya. However, the UNP can become a critical mass for attracting anti-government, anti-Rajapaksa forces only if it is able to set its house in order, provide an effective leadership and prove that it is a united front. Among the JVP there are younger leaders like Tilvin Silva and Bimal Ratnayake.

It should be noted that there has been a transformation of politics across the board, reflecting the changing texture of the emerging leadership. For instance, the prevalent use of Sinhala as the main language at the leadership level, even though their comfort level with English is as good as Sinhala, reflects the changing mores and culture of the political leadership of the future. This is true of the right-of-centre party JHU. The advent of new-generation leaders will be accompanied by Sinhala replacing English as the medium of communication at a personal level too. So will it be in the case of Tamil-speaking communities, where the mother tongue will have greater use, owing to the increasing non-elitist roots of the political leadership at all levels.

The TNA continues to be the umbrella organisation among the Sri Lankan Tamil political parties. The alliance revolves around a few key leaders, such as R Sampanthan, Suresh Premachandran (Alliance spokesperson and leader of the Eelam People's Revolutionary Liberation Front (EPRLF)), V Anandasangaree, leader of the Tamil United Liberation Front (TULF), and Maavai Senathiraja (TULF). Also playing a key role is Douglas Devananda of the Eelam People's Democratic Party (EPDP) which has an identifiable vote-bank going beyond ideological issues. 'Col.' Karuna, or Vinayagamurthy Muralitharan, the former eastern commander of the LTTE and current minister in the ruling SLFP-led government will be important. Eastern province Chief Minister Sivanesathurai Chandrakanthan alias 'Pillaiyan' (former deputy under 'Col.' Karuna) heading the post-war Tamil Makkal Viduthalai Puligal (TMVP) Party that he founded after a split with Karuna is also upcoming. Another leader considered a maverick among the Sri Lankan Tamil politicians is J Sri Ranga, a Jaffna Vellalar who has settled down in Colombo. He won the 2010 parliamentary polls on the opposition UNP-UNF ticket from the Upcountry-stronghold IOTs and won a solitary seat. He has as many enemies in the Tamil polity as he has friends in the Sinhala polity. He has age on his side, which means in the years ahead he has abundant chances to emerge as a major leader in the Sri Lankan politics if he plays his cards carefully.

Among the Muslims, the SLMC continues to be the dominant force. However, there are several splinter groups that have emerged under the leadership of Minister AM Fowzie, a Parsi who is more comfortable in English than Tamil, and AMM Hasbullah and Fariel Ashraff, widow of the SLMC leader. They owe their political identity and support base to specific regions in the east but the latter has left active politics after accepting a gubernatorial assignment in a foreign country, offered by President Rajapaksa following the minimal showing of her party in the 2010 parliamentary polls as an ally.

Among the Upcountry Tamils or the IOTs, the CWC under the leadership of late S Thondaman held its sway for several decades. However, over the years, the Upcountry Tamil polity is being increasingly divided along the lines of caste and is unable to provide a united front, even though four of the CWC candidates won the 2010 parliamentary elections, including S Thondaman's grandson Arumugam Thondaman.

By all indications, Sri Lanka's democratic roots will remain strong. Future politics, however, will be dictated by key factors like the progress made in the reconciliation process, economic development, and the manner in which the political leadership will address issues involving the military.

THE MILITARY LANDSCAPE

The military's role in the campaign against the LTTE has been phenomenal. However, the end of the war has thrown up new challenges for the military such as demobilisation of the big-size military, finding alternative career opportunities once the army is demobilised and maintaining its traditionally apolitical character. In this context, it is pertinent to study the evolving civil-military dynamics to arrive at more fitting conclusions about Sri Lanka's future.

The Sri Lankan military traces its origins to the days of the British Raj. The army is the oldest of the three services and was formally established in 1881 with the rising of the Ceylon Light Infantry Volunteer, which later became the Sri Lankan Light Infantry. Like most colonial-era armed forces, Sri Lanka's too were dominated by the colonial masters; there were a high number of British in the cadre ranks and other decision-making levels. The military gained particular importance during the Second World War when Ceylon was made the Allied Headquarters for the Asian theatre. During the post-war and post-colonial rule, the military transformed itself into more of a ceremonial role given that the newly independent state had limited need for an armed force.

The military of Ceylon, like its British counterpart, was non-political in nature and the trend has by and large continued till date with the only exception being the attempted coup in 1962 by the military reserves.[18] This incident in general was more a result of personal dissent rather than institutional desire to take over power. The failed coup d'état was also dubbed as the 'Colonels coup' since the conspirators belong to that section of the officers that felt disenchanted by the then government's policy of "Sinhalaisation." The military has, otherwise, maintained its apolitical nature despite being heavily involved in internal security issues. However, this incident had created an environment of distrust within the political establishment vis-à-vis the military. As a result, the armed forces of Sri Lanka had faced limitations in the allocation of resources, which would eventually haunt the government.

Threats to Sri Lanka's security have always been from within. The first was the JVP rebellion in the south during the 1970s wherein the army was called in to maintain law and order.[19] As the government was battling the JVP rebels, there was a similar situation brewing in the Tamil-speaking north, which the military battled for the next three decades or so. The fight against LTTE terrorism, unlike the JVP rebellion, required the military to be far more agile and better equipped—in jungle warfare, guerrilla warfare and even urban warfare in the latter part. In fact, the LTTE was much like a regular military force possessing even an air force, however nascent it may have been. Fight against such a well-armed force and the state objective to restrict the militants to the North resulted in the armed forces undergoing a slow but steady transformation from a ceremonial force to a fighting force. While

[18]"How the British Press Saw Mrs Bandaranaike," *Sunday Times*, October 22, 2000, available at http://sundaytimes.lk/001022/plus7.html, (accessed on December 05, 2011).

[19]"Insurgency April 1971," *Sunday Observer*, May 08, 2005, available online at http://www.sundayobserver.lk/2005/05/08/fea01.html (accessed on December 06, 2011).

the transformation to a more professional force did take place, it did not change the basic apolitical character of the military.

The Sri Lankan military's role in politics has always been subservient to the political leadership. The known instances of military participation in public offices have been limited to retired officers and men joining political parties and contesting elections as per norms.

Although former General Sarath Fonseka's attempts to enter politics have been termed as an aberration, he too, like his predecessors, had used political means to fulfil his ambitions. The apolitical nature of the Sri Lankan Army was evident in the election results. Gen. Fonseka could not find particular favour with the army, as was evident with the landslide victory of Rajapaksa, even in his native Ambalagoda town in western Galle district.

The Sri Lankan military today has moved away from an exclusive "elitist-like" force to a more inclusive one, with the common man joining the armed forces at the officer level, climbing up the ladder and reaching the top, as was the case with Sarath Fonseka, for instance. Although Fonseka was made the Army Commander superseding his seniors even before the commencement of Eelam War IV, which was a political decision, the government has moved back to seniority-based promotions, as is seen in the appointment of the current Chief of Army Staff (CoAS). Both of these developments are indicative of the fact that it is the civilian leadership that is in control of the military and that the army has gone back to the barracks, retaining its apolitical character.

A quick glance at the potential leadership in the military over the next fifteen years could help India shape and direct the kind of interaction that the Indian military could potentially pursue. Among the officers who could potentially reach positions of command and decision making in Sri Lanka are the following: Mahinda Hathurusinghe (Commander, Jaffna);

Milinda Peiris (Vice-Chancellor, Kotelawala Defence Academy); Sudantha Ranasinghe (ex-Commissioner-General of Rehabilitation); Mark (Commander, Mullaitivu); and Kamal Guneratne (ex-Commander, Vavuniya). At the level of Brigadier and Colonel-rank officers, who can be expected to reach positions of command, include: Ruwan Kulatunge (ex-Commander, Military Academy); Maithri Dias (Divisional Commander, Mannar); and Eswaran, a Tamil (ex-Chief Instructor, Military Academy).

ROLE OF MILITARY IN POLITICS

It is pertinent to study the role of the military in politics if one were to make a sound judgement of the future of Sri Lankan polity. The size of the army at the beginning of the LTTE conflict was estimated at around 150,000, although this force towards the end of the civil war had become a beefed-up, 250,000-strong force. Available figures show that the Sri Lankan Armed Forces were composed of 185,000 personnel in the Army, 35,000 men in the Navy and 30,000 in the Air Force. There were additionally 50,000 men who were with the Police, and in the case of Sri Lanka, Police has remained under the control and supervision of the Defence Ministry for much of the war years and afterward.

Much of the expansion of the military took place towards the last phase of the ethnic war, under the directive of President Rajapaksa. Today's army is estimated to be one per cent of the island's population. Demobilising such a large force would have several consequences, with alternate employment being one. On the other hand, maintaining such a large military could prove to be a huge drain on the country's economy. In addition, it could potentially create a negative reaction from the population at large, particularly the Tamils. The government sees itself in a Catch-22 situation: it is still worried about a potential regrouping of Tamil militants in the Northeast but, on the other hand, the huge military presence in the areas dominated by the Tamils create insecurity in the minds of the minority population. Incidents such as the one in Jaffna in June 2011 contribute to the suspicion in the minds of Tamil people about the government's intentions.[20]

If the government decides to downsize the military and fails to provide alternate employment to the disbanded military personnel, it could have a negative impact not only in electoral terms but could potentially lay the foundation for a JVP-like militancy in the future. This to a large extent is due to the fact that the major recruitment of the army in the last few years occurred in the Sinhala heartlands, leading to significant improvement in the socio-economic conditions of the people. It should also be kept in mind that army constitutes a large constituency in the electoral politics of Sri Lanka.

A factor that conditions the role of the military in Sri Lankan politics is the nature and character of the new recruits in the army. It is believed that the current generation of military recruits need not necessarily adhere to the professional ethos of the institution and neither are they likely to be politically neutral, which was the case earlier. The concern in the armed forces and the political leadership is more about keeping the large number of inadequately trained soldiers (recruited during the Eelam War IV phase) gainfully occupied to prevent any possibility of mutinous behaviour in the future. The possibility of the military usurping political power or influence is considered remote at this stage.

LTTE RESURGENCE AND THE DEMOBILISATION OF THE ARMED FORCES

The strengthening of the Sri Lankan Armed Forces happened in phases, though the final thrust in this regard was planned during

[20]During a political meeting in Jaffna in June 2011, MPs of the Tamil National Alliance were allegedly attacked by the soldiers of the Sri Lankan Army. Although the army has rejected any involvement, a perception has been created that the military was responsible for the attack. This has added fears in the minds of the minorities deterring them from engaging in political activities.

the peace interregnum provided by the Norway-brokered Ceasefire Agreement (CFA) that commenced in February 2002 and lasted until the end of 2005 and repudiated officially in January 2007, months before the Sri Lankan Armed Forces pushed the LTTE fighters out of the Eastern Province. It is believed that the strategy employed by the armed forces for the Eelam War IV was based on a blueprint prepared by a team of senior officials during the CFA period. This involved increasing the numbers to achieve the traditional 1:10 parity in men required to fight insurgency, taking the country as a single unit with concentration of men and firepower in the North and the East. While it sought peace and used the mode of dialogue, the strategy also did not rule out war given the LTTE's intransigent past to conclude that at some stage a final war would become inevitable and had to be fought to the finish but within an identifiable, and nationally acceptable, timeframe. The choice of a determined commander, who would see through the whole war process, if it could be helped, was a part of such a strategy.

The large-scale recruitment of soldiers to all three services, numbering 100,000 in the first year of the Eelam War IV served multiple purposes. It took the total number to 200,000 apart from the 50,000-strong police force, which continues to come under the Ministry of Defence for overall supervision and coordination (barring a few years prior to 2005). The large-scale recruitment in the army meant that many family incomes had gone up, particularly in the south due to the fixed salary and perks provided by the army. By this approach, the Sri Lankan government managed to check discontentment among families of deceased soldiers or those who went missing.

Yet, the government was ineffective in developing a strategy concerning the demobilisation after the war. This owes to a variety of reasons. Firstly, over the years, all three wings of the armed forces had become fighting machines, given the LTTE's irrepressible ingenuity and constant improvisation of strategies and equipment, which meant that the militant group was working on submarine designs, unmanned and manned aerial missions, about which the military had enough indication from time to time. A battle-hardened institutional mindset began providing for contingencies of any kind where they lacked counter-initiatives in the earlier years of the war. Post-war developments involving the international community's focus on allegations of war crimes and accountability are a case in point. The Sri Lankan establishment at all levels remains convinced that the Diaspora was at work. However, with possible demobilisation in mind but unable to reach there without experimenting, the government has been pressing the armed forces to work on reconstruction projects across the war-torn areas and other developmental projects elsewhere, so that they are not thrown out on the streets in thousands. One aborted attempt in this regard was the government's decision to direct the armed forces to transport and sell vegetables in the markets across the nation, particularly in Colombo, when there was a trade protest in 2011.

Although the troops are currently being diverted to infrastructure projects, it is unlikely that the civilian government will encourage the military to acquire any considerable corporate interest. The army leadership is more concerned about possible indiscipline in the ranks doing some harm than any direct or indirect interference at the command/institutional level, with the existing political leadership and policymaking processes. The leadership is cautious about any possible challenges to the command and control at any future time. But given the financial and other privileges they enjoy, the troops are unlikely to rebel. The army, for its part, is also putting them through additional training protocols to prevent such a possibility.

The armed forces command, however, has one hidden fear: the possibility of the ranks from deep south joining any left militancy of the erstwhile JVP kind. The political leadership shares this fear, independent of any inputs from the armed forces but possibly substantiated by the latter. Both President Rajapaksa and Defence Secretary Gotabya Rajapaksa have aired such fears, the former more openly. This mindset may also explain why they do not want the armed forces camping in the south in large numbers. It can be argued that such 'intelligent explanations' were being offered to ensure that the armed forces were entrenched in the north.

One extraordinary circumstance in which the military may want to intervene could be the area of defence procurement and the commissions that go with it. It is now believed that much of the humiliating defeats suffered by the Sri Lankan Armed Forces in earlier battles against the LTTE owed to some "internal irregularities." Some of the commanders, it was alleged, had ordered the troops not to destroy their weapons before making good their escape when encircled by the LTTE. The credibility of such claims were strengthened after President Rajapaksa, in one of his first few decisions after assuming office in November 2005, appointed a one-man commission to probe past procurements and "suspicious battle-field losses." The assessment is that the Sri Lankan army command still retains much of the British colonial discipline at the officer-rank, and would not want to interfere with civilian administration.

Given the post-war anti-government mood of the international community, there is fear in Colombo that passive militants from the Tamil .community may be emboldened by the prevailing circumstances and encouraged by the Diaspora to regroup. In private, the government do not rule out a future Tamil insurgency minus the LTTE brand of terrorism. Such an insurgency could be confined to state targets including government institutions and political leaders. Total demobilisation is unlikely under circumstances where the political leadership views the world as ganging against Sri Lanka.

Re-emergence of the LTTE in whatever form and name will depend on several factors. These include the level and pace of rehabilitation, and reconstruction and reconciliation effort initiated by the Sri Lankan government. A more critical aspect would, however, be the determination of the divided Diaspora in pushing for the original 'Vaddukottai Resolution' of 1976 for a separate Tamil Eelam, which many of them still swear by. Any future resurgence of the Tamil militancy will also depend on what the West (host countries of Sri Lankan Tamil Diaspora) will do to discourage the Diaspora groups with their activities. The failed Eelam War IV has also helped indoctrinate a new generation of Diaspora Tamils who have been born and brought up in the host countries without any direct influence or impact of the ravages of the war, and its cause and effect. Independent of the willingness of the residual Tamil population left back in Sri Lanka with no hope of finding greener pastures in the absence of familial and societal connections, their long years of hardships could turn many a youth to convince themselves to become a pan-Tamil mercenary dependent on Diaspora resources. This could include Upcountry Tamil youth, whom the LTTE had tried to recruit and whose people were among the worst-hit in the concluding phase of Eelam War IV after they had migrated to the Vanni area through the 1970s and 1980s for a variety of reasons—among them the JVP militant pressure and the earlier Sri Lankan state's disenfranchisement.

The systematic increase in strength and capabilities of the Sri Lankan Armed Forces, through innovation and improvisation, were matched by the relative weakening of LTTE's numbers and capabilities. Borrowing in a way from the LTTE strategy of raising the Sea Tigers naval wing, the Sri Lanka Navy (SLN) too raised a separate unit of fast-attack crafts with the aim of deep penetration with minimal loss of human lives on its side in times of adversarial conditions, including the surprise element that a large vessel could not offer. Post-war, Sri Lankan tactic, experience and expertise are looked upon by various navies of the world, particularly in the context of increasing incidence of piracy in the expanded neighbourhood seas.

Almost from the commencement of hostilities in the 1980s, the Sri Lankan Army had special units for similar tasks, but it was their subsequent experience which made the units more agile and professional. The infant Air Force also acquired teeth, first with Israeli help, and subsequently with China and Pakistan beefing up the capabilities significantly. The intelligence agencies of the government too borrowed heavily on the LTTE tactic in a way, and as a result, there were minimal terror attacks once the Eelam War IV progressed. The process involved de-linking of LTTE supply-chain for terror attacks based on specific information, rather than sticking to the traditional tactic of waiting to capture the entire terror team at one go, which had proved a failure. Post-war, the number of Sri Lankan soldiers has remained high, barring retirement (which will be proportionately low among the ranks owing to the younger age of recruitment in the last years of the war), but so has the grossly inadequate representation of the Tamil minorities.

Victory in the war was not without an economic cost to the Sri Lankan government. The medium- and long-term costs of the war, both in terms of recurring expenditure on the armed forces personnel and repayments for weapons acquired during the war has kept the defence budget spiralling in the post-war years. In October 2011, Sri Lanka proposed a US$ 2.1 billion defence budget for 2012, representing a nearly seven per cent increase compared to US$ 1.7 billion in 2011. Despite increases, for the past few years defence spending has remained at a constant three percent of Sri Lanka's GDP. The 2011 budget amounted to a 6.4 per cent increase over the allocated LKR202 billion (US $1.5 billion) spent in FY10. It also equates to 20 per cent of total national expenditure.[21]

[21] "Sentinel Security Assessment—South Asia," *IHS Jane's Defence*, November 29, 2011, available at http://articles.janes.com/articles/Janes-Sentinel-Security-Assessment-South-Asia/Defence-budget-Sri-Lanka.html, (accessed on March 12, 2012).

Explaining the increase in defence budget for 2012, the government said that expenditures include salaries and allowances for military and police personnel, repayments for military equipment acquired during the long-running conflict, and providing welfare for the families of the "war heroes."

Given suspicions within the Sri Lankan government about short-term internal threats re-emerging in the near future, the military will continue to be part of the decision-making process in Colombo. This will not be seen, however, as interference in policy matters.

IV

Ethno-religious and Demographic Aspects

Like India, Sri Lanka is a multiracial, multilingual and multi-religious country. Its population, according to a 2011 government census, stood at 20.26 million.[22] This population comprises four major ethnic groups: Sinhalese; Sri Lankan Tamils; Indian Tamils; and Sri Lankan Moors or Muslims.

Sri Lanka's ethnic structure has been heavily influenced by colonisation, Western conquests and conversions from India in the north of Sri Lanka. In fact, more than 90 per cent of Sri Lanka's population ultimately has Indian origins, showing the extent to which Sri Lanka's multi-ethnic configuration is determined by its proximity to India and lacking proximity to other nations. Indian migration not only accounts for the bulk of Sri Lanka's population but has also helped engender its majority-minority social structure. The Sinhalese comprise 74.9 per cent of the total population and claim Aryan ancestry, while the Tamils account for 15.4 per cent (Sri Lankan Tamils: 11.2; Indian Origin Tamils: 4.2) and claim Dravidian descent.[23]

Looking at religious denominations, the majority of Sri Lankans are Buddhist. This group is primarily Sinhala-speaking and inhabits the Western, Central, and Southern provinces. They

[22]Department of Census and Statistics, Government of Sri Lanka, "Population Atlas of Sri Lanka 2012," Government of Sri Lanka, available online at http://www.statistics.gov.lk/PopHouSat/PopulationAtla_2012/01_CoverPrefaceAndContents/Pages%20from%20001-DCS_Population_Atlas_of_Sri_Lanka-2012_CD_Version_Final.pdf, (accessed on June 28, 2013).

[23]*ibid.*

are politically and economically dominant in these areas. After the Sinhalese, Hindus (all of them Tamil speaking) are the largest group. They reside primarily in the Eastern and Northern provinces, with the most vibrant cultural and political activity centred on the Jaffna peninsula. Third are the Muslims (mostly Tamil speaking), who live primarily in the Eastern and Southern provinces.[24] Muslims constitute 9.7 per cent of Sri Lanka's population. Finally, the Christians are the island's smallest religious grouping. They speak both Sinhala and Tamil, and comprise roughly 7.4 per cent of the population. This group is geographically dispersed.[25]

Leaving aside caste difference, the Sinhalese are the most ethnically homogenous group. The Tamils are divided along religious lines (Hindu, Muslim, Christian) and caste subdivisions, particularly within the Hindu community, are complex and complicated.

TAMIL ETHNIC DIVISIONS

Modern Sri Lankan Tamil society is essentially a blend of Indian Tamil and Sinhalese culture. Additionally, it incorporates characteristics from other South Indian cultures, such as from Kerala. Sri Lankan Tamils are culturally different from Indian Tamils or Sinhalese. Indian Tamils are descendants of Indian people brought to Sri Lanka by the British in the 1800s as labourers into tea plantations. Such persons constituted 4.2 per cent of the population according to the 2011 Census. There is a certain amount of uncertainty regarding the Tamil-speaking community owing to different national origins (Sri Lanka or India) and religious divisions. Regarding ethnicity, they are divided between "Sri Lankan Tamils" (SLT) and "Upcountry Tamils" of recent Indian origin—also known as "Indian Origin Tamils" (IOT).

[24]Most recently, Muslims are found to be learning Sinhala language given that job opportunities are far higher if one is a Sinhala speaker as against a Tamil speaker.

[25]*ibid.*

Though a common North-East Tamil identity is often presented as a *fait accompli* during ethnic negotiations, traditionally these regions remain separated. The late Tamil leader SJV Chelvanayagam made it his *cause celebre* to hyphenate the grouping. Consequently, a division within the otherwise mono-ethnic LTTE became possible under 'Col.' Karuna in 2003.[26] This was a period of relative peace in the East after the ceasefire agreement came into force in 2002. The split was also fostered by arguments regarding Northern LTTE leadership using Eastern cadres as cannon-fodder.

Regarding Hindu Tamils, the pronounced socio-political identity is linguistic and religious. In the North, Christian socio-political identity is based on language and not religion. Muslims have maintained their religious identity, lately recalling a Persian/Arab past. The Upcountry Tamils or IOTs are concentrated in Sri Lanka's Central Highlands. The IOTs are not accepted as political or social equals by the Sri Lankan Tamil community, who claim to be the natives of the country as the Sinhalese. While Sri Lankan Tamils have political incentives to claim umbilical cord relations with Tamils in India, the IOTs alone can claim legitimate linkages in reality.

The IOTs have a sizeable presence in Colombo and its suburbs, in addition to areas adjoining the Northern and Eastern province highlands.[27] They began by settling in the North, the Vanni forests in particular, either to avoid 1964 Shastri-Sirimavo Pact-instigated expatriation to India or 1970s-era Sinhala nationalist attacks. In the post-war era, it is possible that most Internally Displaced Peoples (IDP) remaining in Northern camps are IOTs

[26]B. Raman, "Split in the LTTE – The Clash of the Tamil Warlords," Paper No. 942, *South Asia Analysis,* available at http://www.southasiaanalysis.org/papers10/paper942.html, (accessed on January 03, 2012).

[27]Department of Census and Statistics, Government of Sri Lanka, "Census of Population and Housing 2001," Government of Sri Lanka, available at http://www.statistics.gov.lk/PopHouSat/PDF/Population/p9p8%20Ethnicity.pdf, (accessed on December 21, 2011).

with neither homes nor jobs. On the other hand, IOT analysts in Colombo claim that substantial numbers of the community had previously identified themselves as Sri Lankan Tamils to avoid expatriation to India.

MUSLIMS

Sri Lanka's Muslims speak either Tamil or Sinhala. Muslims continue to exercise umbilical cord relations with Tamil speakers in Tamil Nadu, through both trade and marriage. However, suspicions owing to ethnic divisions and the subsequent formation of SLMC perhaps contributed to the LTTE-forced exit of 200,000 traditional Muslim residents from the northern Jaffna region in 1990, along with the slaughter of hundreds of Muslims in the East.

The North-East divisions dominating the Tamil linguistic community also exist among the Muslims, which has been a contributing factor to successive SLMC splits. However, Tamil-speaking Muslims particularly dominate middle- and lower-middle-class social life in the national capital of Colombo. The city's demographic and social fabric is, to a large extent, determined by Muslims, Upcountry Tamils, and SLTs who migrated there during period of ethnic conflict. Regarding the negotiated settlement of ethnic issues, Sinhala nationalist elements often refer to Colombo as an example of different communities and linguistic identities that co-exist without LTTE ideology. Analysts often note that SLTs should accept such co-existence in the North and the East.

There is a strengthened degree of identity formation along religious lines among Sri Lanka's Muslims, particularly in the Eastern Province. This reassertion of identity stems primarily from two key triggers. First, the LTTE brutally targeted the community in 1990, following which tens of thousands of Muslims were evicted from the North with little more than Rs 200 and a two-hour notice. Similarly, they were targeted in the East, with worshippers being butchered in mosques. Second, international developments and local consequences stemming from the 9/11 attacks also enhanced Muslim solidarity.

Pakistan ISI's (Inter-Services Intelligence) ability to exploit these sentiments in order to target South India remains a possibility and cannot be discounted. However, within Sri Lanka there is a fear that radicalised Muslim groups could target their own country. Under such a scenario, the fear is also that Muslim extremists could instigate greater radicalisation among Buddhists. Consequently, the state may face the challenge of spiralling communal violence.

Meanwhile, continuing ethnic divisions and weakening Muslim leadership (especially over certain segments of the youth) within Sri Lanka may fuel communal discord. So far, easy access to Gulf employment has kept youths, by and large, from joining militant movements. However, there is a constant fear that some may be misled and cultivated by external actors in the future.

Sri Lanka's ethnic war witnessed large-scale recruitment of Tamil-speaking Muslims into the nation's intelligence service. This made the Tamils bitter, and subsequently, officials became LTTE targets. The wounds might have healed, but the scars remain. This is a wound that pro-LTTE Tamil elements want to open, if only in an attempt to destabilise the government and nation all over again in a nascent attempt at reviving Tamil militancy. The impact of these developments on Sri Lankan radicalism is difficult to predict at this early stage, but its possible adverse consequences cannot be ignored.

BUDDHIST AND CHRISTIAN IDENTITIES

Christians are divided between Tamil and Sinhala speakers. The Christian 'Burghers,' descended from European settlers, are Sinhala speaking. Having been forcibly converted to Christianity by colonial rulers, many Sinhala-Buddhists still carry European names forced on their forefathers. There have been a small but notable number of contemporary re-conversions to Buddhism, particularly with the re-assertion of a 'Sinhala-Buddhist nationalist identity.' This has been particularly true among politicians. For instance, incumbent Minister and Leader of the House in Parliament, Nimal Siripala DeSilva, and the late Junius Richard Jayewardene, a former President, are not Christians but Buddhists.

A recurring question in the constellation of Sri Lankan ethnic issues, particularly within the non-Sinhala-Buddhist minorities, is determining where religion ends and language takes over as a reference point. The reverse may also be possible. The complexities are vexing, especially when one considers that both Tamil-speaking Hindus and Christians identify with common ethnic cause through language, while Tamil-speaking Muslims rely on a religious identity in the national discourse.

This question became more than academic after the LTTE forcibly evicted nearly 200,000 Muslims from the northern Jaffna Peninsula in the early 1990s.[28] An uncomfortable relationship persists between the Tamil National Alliance (TNA) and the Sri Lanka Muslim Congress (SLMC), the largest political grouping on either side of the ethnic equation, but not sole representatives of either community. The two groups have announced on-again-off-again discussions regarding the adoption of a common platform for negotiations with the government, discussions aimed at finding political solutions to ethnic issues.

Traditionally, the SLT community formed the second largest ethno-linguistic group in Sri Lanka after the Sinhala-Buddhists. Buddhists constitute close to three-quarters of the nation's 20 million citizenry.[29] In the tri-ethnic Eastern Province, Tamils,

[28]Nirupama Subramanian, "LTTE and Muslims," *The Hindu*, October 21, 2003, available online at http://hindu.com/2003/10/21/stories/2003102101211000.htm (accessed on February 02, 2012).

[29]Dept. of Census and Statistics, Government of Sri Lanka, "Population Atlas of Sri Lanka 2012," Government of Sri Lanka, available at http://www.statistics.gov.lk/PopHouSat/PopulationAtla_2012/01_CoverPrefaceAndContents/Pages%20from%20001-DCS_Population_Atlas_of_Sri_Lanka-2012_CD_Version_Final.pdf (accessed on June 28, 2013).

Muslims and Sinhala-Buddhists used to each account for roughly one-third of the population, but the figures have since shifted in favour of Tamils, constituting the largest ethnic group in the province. The Muslims, however, have registered the highest population growth rate in the province.[30] For instance, an increase in the population of Muslims is seen in Ampara at 43.6 per cent as against 15.8 per cent for Hindus and 38.6 per cent for Buddhists; and 42.1 per cent for Muslims, 25.9 percent for Hindus and 26.1 percent for Buddhists in Trincomalee.[31]

CASTE, NOT JUST RELIGION

Overall, nothing suggests that Sinhala-Buddhist hegemony will face serious challenges in the foreseeable future. Altogether, the Tamil-speaking minorities account for around a quarter of the nation's population, at best. However, denominational readjustments within the Tamil-speaking population may come to dominate and divert focus from the post-war ethnic discourse, which has been disproportionately centred on Sri Lankan Tamils. This discourse has nearly excluded Upcountry Tamils and Muslims due to several factors.

Unlike the Sri Lankan Tamil community, Upcountry Tamils (first) and Muslims (after) adopted a passive approach to the majority community. This is reflected in their active participation in electoral alliances and acceptance of ministerial berths and other positions of power. It is likely that with the war against the LTTE over, some Sri Lankan Tamils may take pro-government

[30]Dept. of Census and Statistics, Government of Sri Lanka, "Population by ethnic group according to districts, 2012," available at http://www.statistics.gov.lk/PopHouSat/CPH2011/index.php?fileName=pop42&gp=Activities&tpl=3.

[31]Dept. of Census and Statistics, Government of Sri Lanka, "Population Atlas of Sri Lanka 2012," Government of Sri Lanka, available at http://www.statistics.gov.lk/PopHouSat/PopulationAtla_2012/01_CoverPrefaceAndContents/Pages%20from%20001-DCS_Population_Atlas_of_Sri_Lanka-2012_CD_Version_Final.pdf (accessed on June 28, 2013).

positions, with possibly a substantial following from ordinary community members.

Meanwhile, caste has been a defining factor in Sri Lankan politics for both the Sinhalese and Tamils. Govigamas (Sinhala-Buddhists), the land-owning and farming communities, and Vellalars (Sri Lankan Tamils) have historically dominated the social hierarchy. Their dominance has in both cases percolated into the political level. Within the Sinhala-Buddhist community, hill-country Govigamas have held sway over the plains people. Among national leaders, the late SWRD Bandaranaike and the incumbent President Mahinda Rajapaksa are the only notable Govigama leaders from the plains. The former married a hill country Govigama in Sirimavo, who became the Prime Minister after her husband was assassinated by a Buddhist monk.

Slain President Ranasinghe Premadasa, a Hinna, was the only low-caste Sinhala to be elected Head of Government. Former Army commander Sarath Fonseka, who challenged President Rajapaksa in the latter's post-war January 2010 re-election bid, is from the fisher folk 'Karava' community. He lost the election despite early hopes. A section of the UNP, possibly from the low-caste Hinna community, identified with the slain President's son, Sajith Premadasa, who continuously fared badly against incumbent Ranil Wickremesinghe, is an upper caste Govigama. In both cases, the role of caste was central. Among Tamil-speaking Hindus, the SLT continues to look down upon the IOT. SLT leadership's unwillingness to effect complete Tamil social integration, starting with the IOT, continues to be a source of division.

Within the SLT community and (to a lesser extent) the IOTs, caste divisions have been an indicator of social status quo-ism and electoral dynamics. Despite the fact that LTTE leadership was primarily not upper-caste (Prabhakaran was a 'Karayar' fisher) and that LTTE made silent but substantive efforts at social re-engineering within the SLT, caste was one domain where LTTE failed to change the paradigm. The upper caste 'Jaffna Vellalar' community remained mostly untouched by the 30-year war. This, combined with the community's dominance of Diaspora politics and funding, meant that caste divisions remained almost intact. Given the deeply rooted caste divisions, significant changes would take more than a decade to occur. For instance, persons from the 'Jaffna Vellalar' community seldom take brides from the East or northern peninsular states, even if they are originally from the same community. Divisions are still deeper within the Diaspora, which has carried vestiges from the relatively recent past. This is not only true regarding ethnic divisions and politics but also intra-SLT caste factor. Even in the political arena, interaction between the SLTs and IOTs remains limited.

SOCIO-POLITICAL IDENTITIES

Sri Lanka's fractured ethno-religious polity has contributed to coalition politics, which has become the order of the day. Therefore, political parties and 'minority denominations' have been able to acquire a disproportionately high influence in government formation.

In this regard, Muslims and IOTs have been quite active and accommodating. They extend support to the government of the day for several reasons. Since Muslims have a distinct identity, social and political accommodation is necessary, making partnership with the government important. On the other hand, IOTs have sought to work closely with the government in order to ensure economic benefits for their community. Despite having occasional internal rifts, both communities have found ways to work with the government, either through pre-poll alliances or post-poll arrangements.

Sri Lankan Tamil parties became the sole force bent on raising the Tamil issue with Sri Lanka's government. This was primarily an outcome of their lost privileges, privileges enjoyed prior to the 1956 'Sinhala Only' law. These included educational opportunities and government jobs. The only reason for the split within the SLT was that the lower sections of the community could not relate to the elite leadership, who were primarily concerned about the urban middle class.

Regarding caste, a similar situation has unfolded for the Sinhala majority. In an interesting coincidence, the 'Karavar' fisher leadership in the emergence of Prabhakaran among the Tamils was preceded by the Sinhala-Buddhist 'Karavar' community lending leadership to militant JVP in the mid-1960s. In the post-independence era, the JVP emerged as a more radical force, by sticking to class as a differentiating factor.

While forming the SLFP in the early 1950s, SWRD Bandaranaike introduced an ethnic element to the post-independence national discourse. SLFP became identified with education and employment, a mainstay of urban middle class Tamils from the North and (to a lesser extent) the East. Consequently, the traditional left began losing its political base to SLFP. Once ethnic divisions were highlighted, inevitable divisions within the Sinhala-Buddhist nationalist polity could not be avoided. The militant form of the majority community, particularly left-leaning sections, came under the thumb of the backward fisher community. This was an outgrowth of UNP and SLFP leadership by the elite hill country Govigama and plains Govigama, respectively. Each party and group was part of the evolutionary development of popular democracy in Sri Lanka (then Ceylon), which had grown since Sri Lanka became the first South Asian country to introduce the universal adult franchise in 1931.

DEMOGRAPHY AND DEMOCRACY, POST-WAR

Updated post-war electoral rolls in the Northern Province made clear that the voting population in Jaffna was nearly halved over the wartime decades, from nearly 850,000 to 438,512.[32] In future elections, this will mean a fall in parliamentarians elected from the Tamil-majority North, particularly in the Tamil-heavy Jaffna district.

After much delay, the Government has finally launched the electorate delimitation process. Delays have been attributed to the Rajapaksa leadership's inability to push for a change in the country's existing legislative electoral scheme, which is currently a proportional representation system. Howsoever one looks at the issue, the coming fall in SLT legislators can only be delayed, not avoided.

However, the TNA has been making noise about maintaining the status quo. At best, they can arrive at a consensus compromise accompanied by a larger political solution. One method under consideration is postponing delimitation of electorates until after the 2021 census. By that time, post-war demographic patterns and migrations will have stabilised, which would provide a better reflection of Sri Lanka's long-term post-war environment. India's experience in freezing the number of legislative seats since the 1971 delimitation may prove a healthy precedent. However, viewed from the Sinhala-Buddhist political angle and known position of successive Sri Lankan government(s), using India as a guide in this instance is quite unlikely.

As per the 2011 census data, there is an increase in the Muslim population, particularly in the eastern districts. In the tri-ethnic Eastern Province, Muslims could dominate the political scene, possibly to the detriment of Tamils (SLT and IOT) and Sinhalese.

[32]The figure states the number of persons in Jaffna District within the age group of 15 and above. Therefore, the actual voting population will be less than the stated figure. Department of Census and Statistics, Government of Sri Lanka, "Population Atlas of Sri Lanka 2012," Government of Sri Lanka, available at http://www.statistics.gov.lk/PopHouSat/PopulationAtla_2012/01_CoverPrefaceAndContents/Pages%20from%20001-DCS_Population_Atlas_of_Sri_Lanka-2012_CD_Version_Final.pdf (accessed on June 28, 2013).

Whether this situation would assist in integrating the Eastern Tamils and Sinhalese and warding off Muslim electoral dominance remains questionable. In official and security circles, there is concern regarding the increasing number of Muslims in the country. This is heightened by the visible impact of religious fundamentalism in the community, particularly in the eastern interior. Muslims' increasing eagerness to identify with the Gulf-Arab region, especially Wahhabist Saudi Arabia, has also caused concern.

As discussed earlier, Sri Lanka's upper castes have historically dominated politics. The disproportionate upper caste political leadership is increasingly giving way to non-elite representation. The acceptance of President Premadasa in 1989 was merely one indicator, an instance seconded by the Rajapaksa-Fonseka contest. National leadership is increasingly taken up by non-traditional castes and non-elite backgrounds.

Before eventual stabilisation, gradual reorganisation of the Sinhala political scene along caste lines may be a dominant feature of Sri Lanka's politics. The timeframe depends on a number of factors, including internal migration and the emergence of a new leadership generation in various political and community-based parties. The fate of political negotiations over the ethnic issue and its long-term impact on Sri Lankan politics is equally important.

JVP's anticipated weakening also has implications for the future, a weakening dependent on the effectiveness of the two major Sinhala parties. The case is similar for the SLT polity, where upper-caste dominance of TNA/Northern politics may give way to non-elite leadership. Minister and EPDP leader Douglas Devananda remains, among this group, the most visible post-war-era candidate.

Additionally, IOT leadership is currently divided and discredited. However, future IOT leaders may rise from the 'new elite.' If this came to pass, IOT could dominate the entire Tamil community, given the weakness of SLT leadership. For now, IOT political leadership positions are slipping from a small number of Vellalars to the militant intermediary Mukkulathore castes and Dalits.

In conclusion, there are a few broad parameters within which the Rajapaksa government must operate if it remains committed to initiating a socio-political answer to the ethnic problem. Although the Sri Lankan government's 2011 census figures do not indicate a significant decline in Tamil population, scholars and analysts have suggested that the Tamil population could have declined significantly from 11-12 per cent a decade ago to 5-6 per cent today. This decline has two possible sources: war-induced Tamil migration or large-scale loss of life due to the ethnic conflict. In the long run, the Tamil electorate is likely to drop sharply, a circumstance that will greatly impact Sri Lanka's emerging ethnic structure. The level of political strength held by Tamil political parties has already waned, meaning Tamils can no longer push through their demands effectively.

Similarly, many believe that in the absence of the LTTE military might, Tamil influence has greatly diminished. Economically, the Tamil community, hailing from one of the poorest, least developed northern areas, is not faring well. The community's sustenance has been essentially reduced to overseas remittances. Further, post-war northern reconstruction activity has lagged, creating further difficulties for the community. While the Diaspora played a major role in sustaining the LTTE war, its influence has been minimal in the post-war years. Despite the hype surrounding the role of the Diaspora community and external powers in bringing about political devolution and contributing to lasting ethnic solutions, the role of both will be limited in the coming (middle-run) years. However, both groups are likely to be determining forces on Sri Lanka's ethnic question in the long run.

Meanwhile, the Rajapaksa government is riding a wave of triumphalism after its victory over LTTE. However, the government does not discount the possibility of LTTE revival, and therefore the heavy military presence in the North-East. Even as there is little fear of LTTE resurgence, the government has repeatedly asserted the non-existence of ethnic issues, and 'only developmental issues' to focus on. Analysts note that until Rajapaksa is in power, the ethnic issue will remain subservient.

The government must also deal with the Muslim community's role, as their rise is likely to complicate Sri Lankan political dynamics. The rising Muslim community has not only emerged as one of the most enterprising groups on the island, but is also likely to seek greater political representation in the coming years.

LLRC Report and Ethnic Reconciliation

Post-war efforts at political reconciliation have suffered from a variety of factors. While the government displayed callous insensitivity in the aftermath of what was once dubbed an unwinnable war, its reasons for not pushing through a political package in the post-war period owe to the experience of successive governments' unwillingness to implement the India-facilitated 13th Amendment to Sri Lanka's Constitution. The amendment, based on the Indo-Sri Lanka Accord of 1987, guaranteed devolution of power to the provinces over policing and land policy. Moderate pro-LTTE factions remained uninspired. Despite their selective assertion to the contrary, the TNA has also not radically changed its position, wanting the 13th Amendment modified without a separate state. Even if the TNA and the Sri Lankan government were to reach a compromise on the 13th Amendment, it remains unclear whether the Diaspora would support such a move. However, the experience of earlier governments in reaching out to the Tamil community over its leadership (either LTTE or moderates) has not been overly successful.

Though late, the Rajapaksa Government has started talks with the TNA in order to create a political package acceptable to all sections of Sri Lankan society. By implication, this includes all sections of society, not merely the TNA or other pro-government Tamils. While the talks exposed TNA leadership to democratic governance and negotiation, the government has come to the view that long-run national consensus can only be achieved by involving all political players. However, the government's suggestion that a Parliament Select Committee (PSC) be empowered to create a devolution model has few TNA takers.

The strategic choices made by the Rajapaksa government reflected in the delay in the implementation of the 13th Amendment have serious implications. The inaction on the part of the Sri Lankan government has resulted in a sentiment against Colombo within the larger Tamil community. Tamil Nadu is no exception to this. Tamil political parties in India have felt that the peace dividend should have been extended to the Tamils in the North and East. Creation of a positive and constructive mood in Tamil Nadu should have been a priority for Colombo. Gotabaya Rajapaksa's recent comment at a lecture at the Kotewala Defence University that "Tamil Nadu's attitude towards Sri Lankan government could be a serious threat to Sri Lanka's security and perhaps even to sovereignty" reflects the negative impact of the government's policies.[32a] The negative sentiment among the Tamil Diaspora, particularly in Malaysia, Australia, Canada, and Europe, could also become a problem for Sri Lanka.

In this backdrop, one must view the recent report from the Lessons Learnt and Reconciliation Commission (LLRC), which was appointed by the Rajapaksa regime to counter mounting international pressure regarding accountability for war-time crimes and human rights violations. The LLRC report was preceded by recommendations from the three-member expert panel appointed by U.N. Secretary-General Ban Ki-moon, who felt that the Rajapaksa Government had not kept its promises.

[32a]N.S. Venkataraman, "Sri Lanka's Relations with India and China," *The Sri Lanka Guardian,* June 15, 2013.

However, the international discourse (including the ones at the UNHRC in Geneva) has mostly revolved around the LLRC report, not on the Darusman Report of U.N. Experts, which Ban had forwarded to Geneva. The LLRC Report, accepted by the Sri Lankan government, recommended investigations into specific complaints regarding disappearances and killings of Tamils during Eelam War IV. The armed forces have since created a special panel to look at these cases, and the government has announced that government lawyers will not defend those against whom charges were made. However, it remains unclear whether the accused would be tried in civilian or military courts, if that stage is reached.

The LLRC Report also discussed political reconciliation and power-devolution, although the current government seems committed to its PSC-related approach. In its interim report, the seven-member commission commended the 'three-language formula,' which has been under discussion for several years now.[33] The Sri Lankan government has asked for India's assistance in this regard. Rajapaksa has, in fact, created a Presidential Task Force, which coordinated its efforts with the Central Languages University of Hyderabad (routed through the Indian government).

However, on the critical accountability issue, the LLRC has not made any recommendations regarding higher-echelon leadership's responsibility for war-crimes. LLRC failed to indict or imply the involvement of any political, bureaucratic or command-level military officers. Also, the government has clearly indicated its willingness (through the LLRC Report) to implicate and punish anti-LTTE Tamil Minister Douglas Devananda and his EPDP for targeting adversaries with war-time paramilitaries. In other words, the current government is willing to lay blame on opposing political parties for war-time crimes without shining any spotlight on its own actions.

[33]The trilingual formula would require minority Tamils to learn Sinhala and the Sinhalas to learn Tamil, with English continuing to be the link language. While this is a step forward, this scheme does not bring the state any closer to finding a solution to the ethnic conflict.

V

Socio-Economic and Commercial Aspects

The Sri Lankan economy has seen steady GDP growth since 2002. The year 2009 was a notable exception, although this is attributable to the global economic crisis. Interestingly, even during peak war years (2006-08), GDP growth was stable, averaging at 6 to 7 per cent. Following the brief GDP fall of 2009, Sri Lanka's economy rebounded in 2010 with GDP growth of 8 per cent (Figure 1).[34] The reasons for this uptick are manifold: the end of conflict in 2009; declining interest rates; expansionary fiscal policy; large inflows of foreign capital; an increase in tourism; and a boom in agriculture.

Figure 1: Sri Lankan GDP Growth since 2001

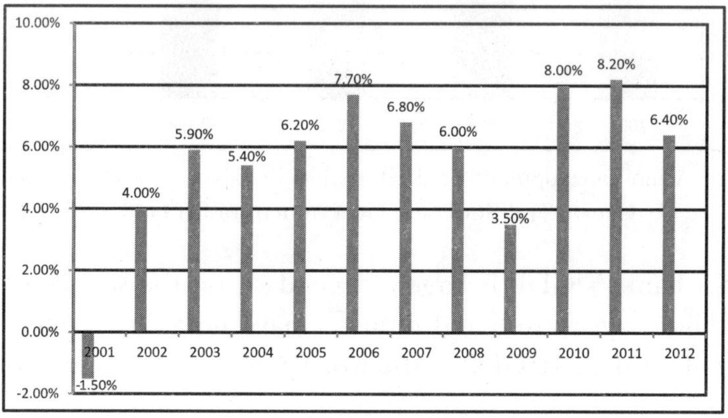

Source: World Bank and Department of Census and Statistics, Government of Sri Lanka.

[34]Own composition based on data from: http://data.worldbank.org/indicator/NY.GDP.MKTP.KD.ZG.

Generally, the sectoral composition of the Sri Lankan economy represents a modern structure, with the service sector being its biggest contributor followed by industry and, lastly, the agricultural sector (Figure 2). The service sector's contribution increased from 52.6 per cent in 2001 to 57.8 per cent in 2010. Simultaneously, the share of the agricultural sector dipped from 16.8 per cent in 2001 to 12.8 per cent in 2010. The contribution of the industrial sector, meanwhile, continues to be relatively stable, at 30.6 per cent in 2001 and 29.4 per cent in 2010.[35]

Figure 2: Sector Breakdown of Sri Lanka's GDP

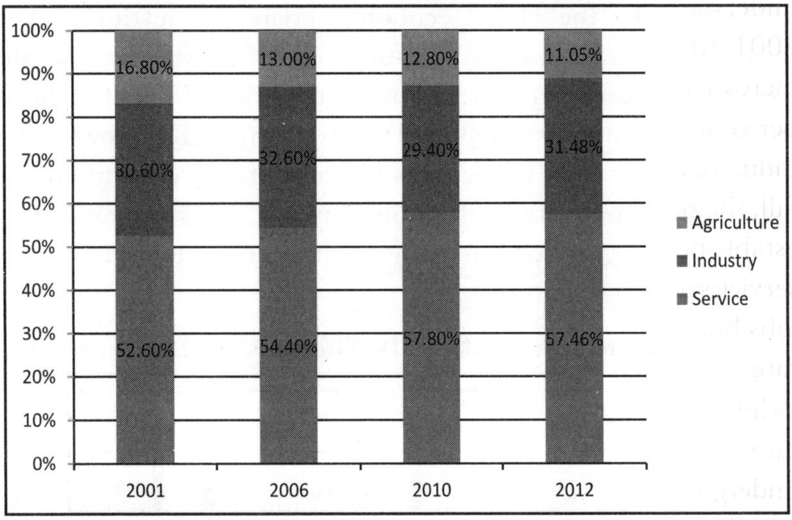

Source: Asian Development Bank Statistical Database and Department of Census and Statistics, Government of Sri Lanka.

Sri Lanka's GDP is largely dependent on the service sector, while both agriculture and industry have notably declined as a share of 2001-2010 GDP.[36] Also worth noting: contribution of the

[35]ADB statistical database system, available at https://sdbs.adb.org/sdbs/index.jsp.

[36]The drop noted in agriculture (4 per cent) is significantly larger than the drop in the industrial sector's share (1.2 per cent). *ibid.*

service sector to Sri Lanka's GDP stands higher than its contribution to the Indian economy.[37]

The central role played by services in Sri Lanka's economy is not merely measured by its contribution to GDP but also by employment generated. In 2010, 42.9 per cent of Sri Lanka's population was employed in the service sector.[38] While there have been minor variations in labour employed by sectors, the service sector consistently (and by a wide margin) remains Sri Lanka's largest employer.

A look at Sri Lanka's overall employment rate provides a better understanding of the service sector's role in its economy. From 2001-2010, the employment rate showed improvement. The increase in the employment rate from 93.5 per cent in 2006 to 95 per cent in 2010 is particularly significant.[39] During these years, industrial sector employment declined by 2 per cent.[40] Despite the fall, the positive growth recorded by Sri Lanka's employment rate establishes the robustness of the country's largest employer. The service sector not only managed to cover the fall in industrial sector jobs but also made possible overall national employment growth rate.

While the country's overall employment rate changed positively during the assessed years, the employment gender ratio did not undergo "major" changes. From 2001-2010, the employed population was male dominated.[41] However, changes witnessed in Sri Lanka's gender profile across age groups from 2001-10 have been significant. Figure 3 illustrates how starting from the age 25-

[37] See *CIA Factbook*, available at https://www.cia.gov/library/publications/ the-world-factbook/geos/ce.html.

[38] ADB statistical database system available at https://sdbs.adb.org/sdbs/ index.jsp.

[39] *ibid.*

[40] *ibid.*

[41] *ibid.*

29 ranging to 75 and over, women are slowly but surely outpacing the number of men.[42]

Figure 3: Gender-based Age Representation of Sri Lanka's Population

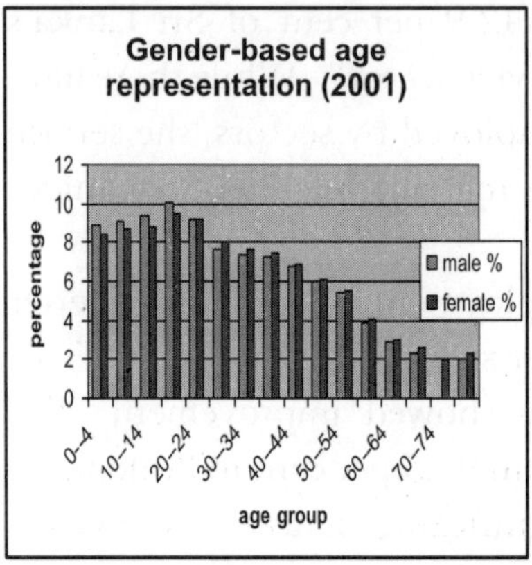

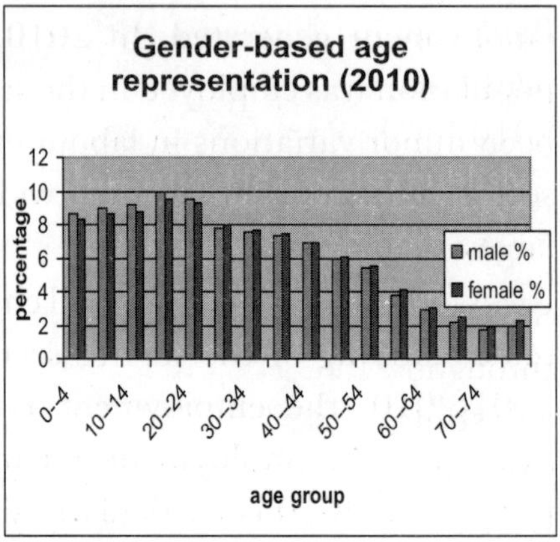

Source: Own calculation of data available in "Sri Lanka Labour Force Survey," Annual Report, 2010, available at http://www.statistics.gov.lk/samplesurvey/LFS_Annual%20Report_2010.pdf.

Additionally, Sri Lanka will be challenged going forward by a vast increase in average life expectancy, now up to 75 years. To its credit, Sri Lanka has achieved one of the highest life expectancies both among developing and many developed nations. The increasing life expectancy success story will test Sri Lanka. Supplemented by an increasing female population from the age of 25 (Figure 3), life expectancy increases, many predict, will create a slowdown in labour force growth and an eventual contraction by 2030.[43] Moreover, Sri Lanka has recorded the

[42]Own calculations based on information given in: http://www.statistics.gov.lk/samplesurvey/LFS_Annualpercent20Report_2010.pdf Department of Census and Statistics.

[43]*Population Aging and the Labour Market, The Case of Sri Lanka,* The World Bank, available at http://siteresources.worldbank.org/SOCIALPROTECTION/Resources/SP-Discussion-papers/Labor-Market-DP/0821.pdf, abstract.

highest spending on civil service pensions in the region. These pensions account for almost 10 per cent of government revenues. Consequently, the pension scheme has been a main source of the country's perennial budget deficit, as noted by a 2007 World Bank report. According to Sri Lanka's Department of Pensions, pensioners increased by almost 32 per cent between 1998 and 2010.[44]

TRADE

Sri Lanka has experienced a persistent merchandise trade deficit throughout the past decade. In 2010, Sri Lanka's exports grew at an estimated 17.5 per cent, while imports grew by 24 per cent. Consequently, the country ended 2010 with a trade deficit of U.S. $5 billion. However, in 2011 export growth was estimated at 8.6 per cent, while imports were believed to have increased by 7.7 per cent. Import growth is estimated at 10.1 per cent, which once again means a significant trade deficit. In 2010, the ratio of exports to GDP stood at about 10 per cent and 18.5 per cent in 2011. Sri Lanka is highly export-dependent, with a higher exports to GDP ratio than larger economies in South Asia, such as India (16.2 per cent) and Pakistan (15.1 per cent).[45]

EXPORTS AND IMPORTS

Sri Lanka's major export destinations as of 2010 are E.U. (35 per cent); U.S. (21.1 per cent); U.K. (12.3 per cent); India (12 per cent); and Italy (5.6 per cent). Together, these economies

[44]Department of Pensions, Government of Sri Lanka, Available at http://www.pensions.gov.lk/index.php?option=com_content&view=article&id=95&Itemid=53&lang=en.

[45]All own calculations based on data from *CIA factbook,* available at https://www.cia.gov/library/publications/the-world-factbook/geos/ce.html, https://www.cia.gov/library/publications/the-world-factbook/geos/in.html and https://www.cia.gov/library/publications/the-world-factbook/geos/pk.html.

accounted for 86 per cent of overall exports (See Figure 7). In 2010, textiles amounted to 63 per cent of total exports to these five trade partners.[46]

Figure 4: Sri Lanka's Direction of Trade

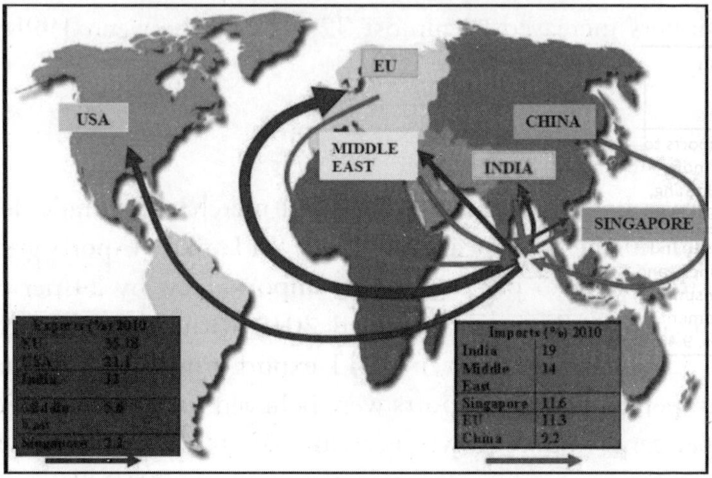

Source: 2011 Export Achievements, Department of Commerce, Sri Lanka.

Given the particularly sensitive nature of clothing to consumer demand, Sri Lanka realises its needs to diversify its export structure and focus on developing a commensurate market for its fastest growing sector, services. Moreover, given that four out of the five export nations/partners (U.S., E.U., U.K., and Italy) are currently struggling through economic malaise, trade diversification has become imperative. An exception is Sri Lanka's fourth biggest export partner (India) with which the country has a sufficiently diversified export structure (Figure 5).[47]

On the other hand, Sri Lanka's import structure seems more diversified around four equally portioned goods categories.

[46]Own composition based on data from Sri Lanka Customs, National Gem and Jewellery Authority, Central Bank of Sri Lanka.

[47]Own composition and calculations based on the data from: http://www.trademap.org/countrymap/Product_SelCountry_TS.aspx.

Regarding India, Sri Lanka's biggest import partner, the country mainly imports agricultural products and raw materials (27 per cent), machinery and transport equipment (25 per cent) and mineral fuels and oil (16 per cent).[48]

Figure 5: Exports to India 2010

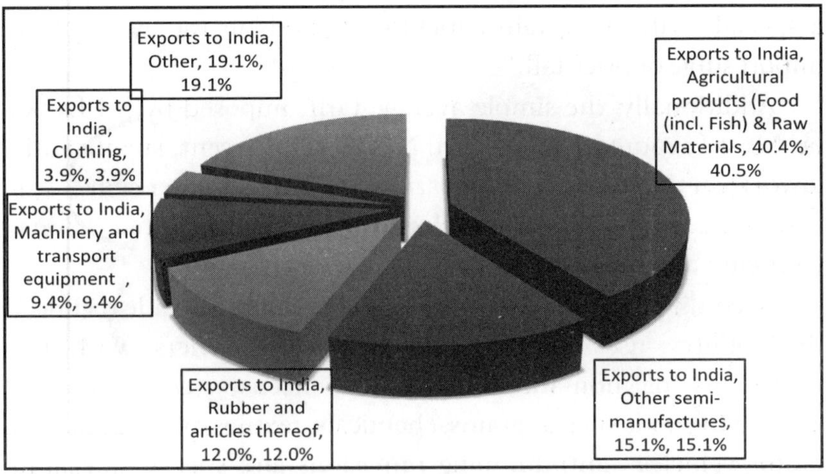

Source: Own calculations of data given in "Trade Map," International Trade Centre, available at: http://www.trademap.org/index.aspx?ReturnUrl=%2fProduct_SelCountry_TS.aspx.

The high level of Indian agricultural imports is worth noting because agriculture contributes roughly 13 per cent of Sri Lanka's overall GDP (Figure 2). Additionally, it still employs 33 per cent of the national labour force.[49] Moreover, Sri Lanka's still strong rural society depends on functioning, productive agricultural and livestock activities. Nevertheless, lacking industrialisation and mechanisation within this sector has caused the WTO (Sri Lanka has held membership since January 01, 1995) to declare Sri Lanka a net food importing developing country (NFIDC).

[48] *ibid.*

[49] ADB statistical database system available at https://sdbs.adb.org/sdbs/index.jsp.

Sri Lanka's Doha Round position includes enhancing food supply, protecting national (particularly subsistence) farmers from cheap agricultural imports, and safeguarding employment opportunities, especially for the rural poor.[50] Understandably, Sri Lanka strongly insists on the allowance of SSMs, or special safeguard measures, designed to protect poor farmers by imposing a special tariff on certain agricultural goods in the event of an import surge or price fall.[51]

Additionally, the simple average tariff imposed by Sri Lanka on Most Favoured Nations (MFN) is 11.5 per cent, significantly lower than the Indian average tariff. However, 11.5 per cent is still higher than many other developed export nations, like China, Germany, and the U.S.[52]

According to the WTO's analysis of Sri Lanka's trade regime,[53] the country uses very limited non-tariff barriers, with the exceptions of non-automatic export license requirements—applied to goods such as grains, chemicals, textiles, petroleum, and motor vehicles—anti-dumping provisions and special safeguard measures. There are also 103 technical regulations identified by the WTO, which concluded that Sri Lanka generally follows international guidelines.

Sri Lanka's oil import structure is particularly relevant. Due to a lack of natural resources, Sri Lanka remains highly dependent on crude oil imports. In 2009, for instance, 92 per cent of annual oil

[50]Kelegama, S. (2006): WTO Hong Kong Ministerial Outcome and Sri Lanka. Paper presented at a seminar on Achievements at the Recent WTO Ministerial Conference in Hong Kong, January 24, 2006 organized by the National Chambers of Commerce of Sri Lanka (NCCSL), Colombo.

[51]As per Sri Lankan Ministry of Commerce (2011): 2011 Export achievements available at http://www.doc.gov.lk/web/pdf/export_achievement_2011.pdf.

[52]As per The World Bank. World Trade Indicators 2009/10, http://info.worldbank.org/etools/wti/3b.asp?pillarID=1&indList=66&indList=13&indList=14&indList=15&cList=41&cList=71&cList=86&cList=176&cList=201&regionID=r8&periodID=16.

[53]http://www.wto.org/english/tratop_e/tpr_e/s237_sum_e.pdf.

consumption (33,500,000 barrell) was imported.[54] Figure 6 highlights the main trading partners on whom Sri Lanka depends for mineral, fuel, oil and distillation product imports.[55]

Figure 6: Import of Minerals, Fuels, Oil, Distillation Products—the TOP 5 in 2010-Shares Per Good

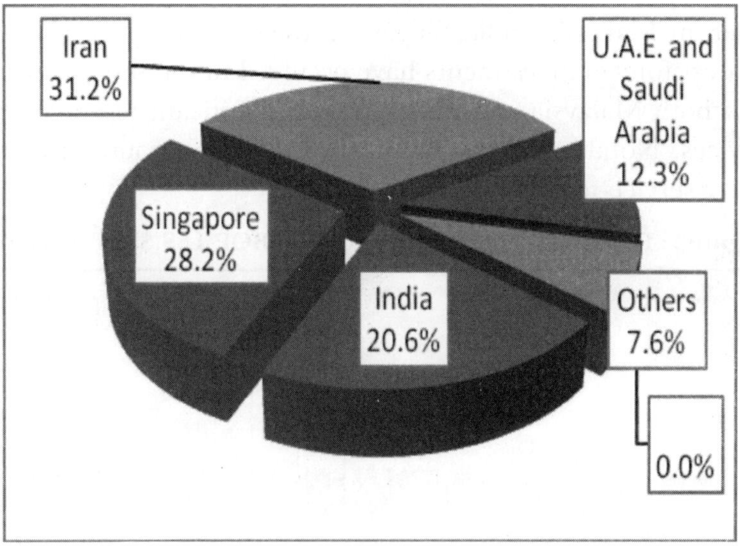

Source: Own calculations of data given in "Trade Map," International Trade Centre, available at http:/www.trademap.org/index.aspx?ReturnUrl=%2Product_SelCountry_TS.aspx.

THE IMPACT OF FDI ON SRI LANKA'S ECONOMY

Sri Lanka's Board of Investment managed to promote FDI inflows by projecting an image of Sri Lanka as an open economy, a regional trading hub providing strategic access to the Indian market. Indeed, FDI inflows increased steadily, tripling from U.S. $230

[54]Own calculations based on data from *CIA factbook:* https://www.cia.gov/library/publications/the-world-factbook/geos/ce.html.

[55]Own composition and calculations, based on the data from: http://www.trademap.org/countrymap/Product_SelCountry_TS.aspx.

million in 2004 to U.S. $750 million in 2008. However, following the economic crisis, FDI inflows fell to U.S. $404 million in 2009. While this number rebounded to U.S. $478 million in 2010, Sri Lanka has been unable to achieve pre-crisis levels of investment (Figure 7).[56]

Sri Lanka's top sources of FDI in recent years, in descending order, are Malaysia, India, Singapore, the U.K., and Australia. The greatest foreign investments have occurred in the services sector, with both Malaysia and India pouring significant resources into services. Notably, telecommunications alone accounts for over half of service-related FDI.[57]

Figure 7: Foreign Direct Investment, Net (BOP, U.S.$) in Sri Lanka

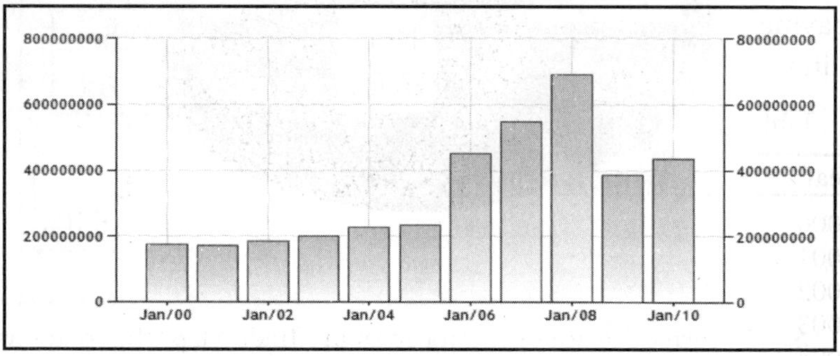

Source: http://www.tradingeconomics.com.

TRENDS IN DEFENCE EXPENDITURE AND ITS IMPACT ON THE SRI LANKAN ECONOMY

Between 2006 and 2008, Sri Lanka's military spending increased from 2.8 to 3.71 per cent in 2008 (Table 1). Sri Lanka also notched the highest percentage (GDP) of military spending within South Asia from 2008-2009.[58] Following the end of the civil war in 2009,

[56]*World Investment Report 2011,* UNCTAD available at http://www.unctad-docs.org/files/UNCTAD-WIR2011-Full-en.pdf.

[57]A survey of foreign direct investment in G-15 countries available at http://www.g15.org/workingpaper7.pdf.

[58]SIPRI Military Expenditure Database available at http://www.sipri.org/research/aronaments/milex/milex_database.

total military spending decreased by 6.8 per cent, reflecting in a fall of military spending to 2.7 per cent of GDP in 2010.

However, this fall was short-lived. In 2011, with a 2.9 per cent share in the country's GDP, the military expenditure rose by 2 per cent. Further, although the defence budget (U.S. $1.5 billion) reduced by 9.5 per cent in 2012, the Defence Ministry has announced its decision to increase the military budget to U.S. $2.1 billion in 2013. Sri Lanka's government chalked up the defence budget increases to augment salaries and allowances for military and police personnel, repayments for military equipment acquired during the long-running LTTE conflict, and money allotted for the families of 'war heroes.'[59] Preoccupied by elections in 2010, the government had been unable to cater to these repayment needs, which contributed to that year's decreased military expenditure.

Table 1: Sri Lanka's Military Expenditure as Per Cent of GDP

Year	US $ Million	% Increase	% of GDP
2000	1675*	4.794*	5.0*
2001	1398*	-16.54*	4.3*
2002	1157*	-17.24*	3.3*
2003	1040*	-10.11*	2.9*
2004	1159	11.44	3.0
2005	1073	-7.42	2.6
2006	1239	15.47	2.8
2007	1517	22.43	3.3
2008	1737	14.5	3.7
2009	1794	3.28	3.6
2010	1672	-6.8	3.1
2011	1706	2.03	2.9
2012	1543	-9.55	2.4

*SIPRI estimates, based on 2011 constant.
Source: SIPRI Military Database available at
http://www.sipri.org/research/armaments/milex/milex_database

[59]Jane's Intelligence and Insight available at http://articles.janes.com/articles/Janes-Sentinel-Security-Assessment-South-Asia/Defence-budget-Sri-Lanka.html and "Sri Lanka Raises Taxes to Boost Defence Spending," *DAWN*, November 08, 2012, available at http://beta.dawn.com/news/762519/sri-lanka-raises-taxes-to-boost-defence-spending.

PROVINCE LEVEL TRENDS

(a) Economy

The Western Province—which includes Sri Lanka's political and economic capital, Colombo—generates the lion's share of the country's total GDP. However, in a comparison of provincial GDP shares in 2006 and 2009, the contribution of the Western Province decreased by five per cent, in favour of five other provinces. Although Sri Lanka's GDP still strongly depends on the Western province, shifting trends demonstrate that the other provinces are increasing in relative economic significance. The Sri Lankan economy, in geographical terms, is becoming increasingly diversified.

Nevertheless, a deeper look at sectoral composition by provinces reveals tremendous intra-country variations. In 2009, the Northern Province had the largest share of service sector contributions to GDP (74 per cent). On the other hand, the Northern Province accounts for the lowest provincial share of industry (8 per cent) and lowest contribution to overall GDP (3 per cent).[60]

Moreover, the agricultural split among the provinces ranged from three to 30 per cent in 2009. Except for the Western Province, agriculture accounts for a share of provincial GDP far above the national average of 13 per cent. The non-agrarian Western Province accounts for nearly 50 per cent of national GDP, so agriculture's share in GDP remains relatively low, not reflecting its importance in other provinces. Sri Lanka is much more an agrarian economy than national numbers indicate.

A major transformation process in Sri Lanka is underway. If one compares the sector significance of four provinces (Southern, Sabara-Gamuwa, Central and North-Western) in 2002 and 2009,

[60]Own composition based on the published data of the Central Bank of Sri Lanka (2010), *Annual Report 2010*.

major differences are discernable.[61] Within the cluster, agriculture's average share of the provincial economy decreased from 33.5 per cent in 2002 to 18.5 in 2009. Additionally, the industrial sector increased from 23.5 to 30 per cent, while services went from 42.5 to 51 per cent. This rapid, ongoing process reflects a shift from a more labour-intensive agro focus to a less labour-dependent service sector. Two major questions arise:

1. Can the government accommodate workers left unemployed due to the transition process?

2. How will the growing population of older people and women be accommodated by this shift?

(b) Demographics

The Western Province of Sri Lanka remains the most densely populated, recording the highest population figures from 2001-2010.[62]

Table 2: Total Population of the Provinces (2001-2010) (In thousands)

Province	2001	2006	2010	2012
Central	2,424	2576	2689	2557
Eastern	1419	1525	1561	1547
Northern	1041	1111	1193	1060
North Central	1104	1172	1240	1259
North Western	2170	2266	2342	2372
Sabaragamuva	1802	1884	1943	1919
Southern	2278	2392	2494	2466
Western	5381	5669	5865	5837
Uva	1178	1263	1326	1259

Source: Department of Census and Statistics, Government of Sri Lanka.

[61]They almost equally account altogether for 36 per cent of the overall GDP and after the Western Province these are the highest contributors to the country's GDP. As per *CIA factbook* estimations (2011), available at https://www.cia.gov /library/publications/the-world-factbook/geos/ce.html.

[62]Department of Census and Statistics, Government of Sri Lanka available at http://www.statistics.gov.lk/PopHouSat/Mid percent20Yearpercent 20Population/midyearsex&district.pdf.

A gender breakdown of the total population shows that the majority of Sri Lanka's provinces record higher percentages of women, as compared to men, from 2001 to 2010. The exceptions were Uva and North Central.[63] The North Central Province recorded the lowest female population during the same period. The Eastern Province had the most notable change in its year-on-year gender composition. While the province recorded a higher percentage of males to females in 2001 and 2006, this was reversed in 2010. Women constitute 51.1 per cent of the province's population (Appendix 1). Furthermore, the Northern and Eastern Provinces underwent major changes in their female population from 2006-2010. A growth rate of 9.4 per cent was recorded in the Northern Province, compared to 5.6 per cent in the Eastern.[64]

(c) Literacy

Regarding provincial literacy, Uva and the North Central Provinces—which recorded lower female populations (See Appendix 1)—stand out also having lower literacy rates, as compared to the other provinces. In Uva, the literacy rate increased from 85.6 per cent in 2001 to 86.6 per cent in 2010 but remained the lowest in any province. Further, the North Central Province recorded a declining literacy rate, a drop from 90.3 per cent in 2001 to 89.4 per cent in 2010.[65] Although the fall in literacy was marginal, it must be highlighted because this was the only province where literacy declined in a 2010 measurement.

[63]While females accounted for 48.6 per cent of North Central's population, they accounted for 49.8 per cent of Uva's population in 2010. ibid

[64]ibid.

[65]Labour Force Survey, Government of Sri Lanka available at http://www.statistics.gov.lk/samplesurvey/LFS_Annual%20Report_2010.pdf.

Table 3: Number of Pupils in Provinces (2003-2010)

Province	2003	2006	2010	2011
Central	530	504	522	523
Eastern	365	372	385	384
Northern	**260**	**266**	**240**	246
North Central	**262**	**248**	**248**	259
North Western	470	457	473	476
Sabaragamuva	382	362	368	368
Southern	520	495	504	507
Western	863	858	916	927
Uva	290	277	277	279
Total	**3942**	**3838**	**3933**	**3969**

Note: Schools in Kilinochchi & Mullaitivu districts of the Northern Province were temporarily closed at the census date in 2009.

Source: Economics and Social Statistics of Sri Lanka 2012, Central Bank of Sri Lanka, Volume XXXIV, pp. 138, available at: http://www.cbsl.gov.lk/pics_n_docs/10_pub/_docs/statistics/other/econ_&_ss_2012.pdf.

As shown in the table, the number of pupils in the North Central Province fell over the 2003-2010 period.[66] The decline in Northern Province pupils, largely attributable to its being the Eelam War IV epicentre, is likely to continue in the near future. This trend is due to the fact that the primary economic activities of the region are stunned as a result of the war and the government is yet to come up with new income generation models for the region.

(d) Poverty and Access

Table 4 illustrates provincial poverty numbers. It gives an overall positive impression of Sri Lanka's economy and development trajectory. From 2001-2010, there has been a marked fall in

[66]Central Bank of Sri Lanka, *Economics and Social statistics of Sri Lanka*, available at http://www.cbsl.gov.lk/pics_n_docs/10_pub/_docs/statistics/other/econ_&_ss_2011.pdf.

poverty rates. The trends in two provinces draw particular attention. From 2006-2010, Eastern Province poverty rose from 10.8 per cent to 14.8 per cent. That province also had the highest absolute number of persons in poverty. Uva, on the other hand, noted the greatest decline in poverty, from 31.8 per cent to 13.7 per cent between 2002 and 2010.[67]

Table 4: Poverty Ratio by Province

Province	2002 (per cent)	2006/07* (per cent)	2009/10 (per cent)
Central	20.8	22.3	9.7
Eastern	-	10.8	**14.8**
Northern	-	-	12.8
North Central	18.1	14.2	5.7
North Western	22.3	14.6	11.3
Sabaragamuva	28.9	24.2	10.6
Southern	23.6	13.8	9.8
Western	9.2	8.2	4.2
Uva	**31.8**	**27**	**13.7**

*Data for 2006/07 excludes Northern Province and Trincomalee district in Eastern Province.

Source: Household Income and Expenditure Survey, Sri Lanka.

The provinces also recorded an increase in mean household income from 2002-2010. However, the 43.7 per cent increase in North Central Province household income should be noted. Not only did the province record the largest increase in household income over the period, but rising income paralleled falling literacy rates.[68] Uva witnessed a slow but steady rise in mean household

[67]Ministry of Finance and Planning, Government of Sri Lanka, *Household and Income Expenditure Survey, Final Report*, available at http://www.statistics.gov.lk/HIES/HIES2009_10FinalReport.pdf.

[68]Department of Census and Statistics, Government of Sri Lanka, *National Accounts of Sri Lanka 2009*, available at http://www.statistics.gov.lk/national_accounts/Annual2009/index.pdf.

income from 2002-2010. The Western Province, as observed in measurements of other social indicators (literacy rate: 95.7 per cent, poverty head count: 4.2 per cent),[69] continues to have the best social conditions and highest household incomes (Appendix 2).[70]

Provincial data also reflects decent access essentials, such as safe drinking water and electricity. The Central Province had the lowest access to safe drinking water in 2010, at 72.1 per cent. The Eastern Province is less well-electrified (Table 5), as only 70.6 per cent of households had electricity in 2009. In particular, Uva has limited quantities of both. In 2009, Uva was third from the bottom in safe drinking water access (78.3 per cent) and last in terms of electrification (75.5 per cent).[71] Uva's lack of access to these essentials is the primary factor responsible for its slow improvement in social conditions from 2001 to 2010.

Table 5: Access to Electricity, by Province (%)

Province	2006	2009
Central	78.2	89.6
Eastern	68	70.6
Northern	*	48.2
North Central	69.1	82.3
North Western	70.7	92
Sabaragamuva	71.3	83.5
Southern	84.4	95.6
Western	92.8	98.1
Uva	**69.2**	**75.5**

Source: United Nations Development Programme (UNDP), *Millennium Development Goals Country Report: Sri Lanka* (Colombo: UNDP, 2005). Data is unavailable for northern provinces (Jaffna, Mannar, Vavuniya, Mullaitivu, Kilinochchi).

[69]Department of Census and Statistics, Government of Sri Lanka, *Household Income and Expenditure Survey*, available at http://www.statistics.gov.lk/HIES/HIES2009_10FinalReport.pdf.

[70] *ibid.*

[71]Department of Census and Statistics, Government of Sri Lanka, available at http://www.statistics.gov.lk/MDG/Indicators percent20New/indica30.pdf; http://www.statistics.gov.lk/HIES/HIES2009_10FinalReport.pdf.

ASPECTS OF ECONOMIC DIPLOMACY AND ITS IMPACT ON EXTERNAL RELATIONS

With implementation of Sri Lanka's economic policy strategy, the composition and form of external development assistance have substantially changed. As *Sri Lanka: The Emerging Wonder of Asia (Development Policy Framework of the Government of Sri Lanka)* makes apparent, Sri Lanka has officially graduated to the status of a middle-income country.[72]

Sri Lanka receives a substantial amount of foreign assistance. Significant donors include China, the World Bank, the Asian Development Bank, Japan, and others. In 2010, financial disbursements amounted to U.S. $2,121 million. Notably, there has been a 30 per cent increase in foreign financial assistance since 2009.[73]

China has been a major lender for infrastructure projects, such as a new port, a coal power plant, and roads. Iran has also been a major lender, committing U.S. $450 million for the Uma Oya multipurpose irrigation project and U.S. $111 for rural electrification. Moreover, Iran provides an interest-free credit facility for oil imports and has promised assistance for the modernisation of Sri Lanka's only oil refinery, although no firm commitments are yet in place. Although India has also contributed by providing loans for Sri Lanka's railway sector, its assistance lags behind China's.[74] For India, Sri Lanka's financial dependence on China has worrisome strategic implications.

[72]Department of Financial Planning, Government of Sri Lanka, *Sri Lanka: Emerging Wonder of Asia* available at http://www.treasury.gov.lk/publications/mahindaChintanaVision-2010full-eng.pdf.

[73]Ministry of Finance and Planning, Government of Sri Lanka, *Annual Report 2010* available at http://www.treasury.gov.lk/reports/annualreport/AnnualReport2010-eng.pdf

[74]U.S. Department of State, available at http://www.state.gov.

IMPACT OF INDIA'S ECONOMIC GROWTH ON SRI LANKA AND LEVERAGE PROVIDED TO IMPROVE BILATERAL TIES

Growing economic linkages define the Sri Lanka-India relationship. Sri Lanka's exports to India reached Sri Lankan Rs 52,686 million in 2010, an increase of 3.53 per cent over four years. Similarly, India's exports to Sri Lanka recorded rapid growth, reaching Sri Lankan Rs 2,905,23 million in 2010, a rise of 28.6 per cent from 2006. Part of this growth is a consequence of the India-Sri Lanka bilateral Free Trade Agreement (FTA) of 2000. Incidentally, this was India's first bilateral FTA.[75]

India was also one of the top five sources of Sri Lankan investment in 2009, accounting for 6.5 per cent of total FDI stock. According to Sri Lanka's Board of Investment, over half of Indian investments in the South Asian Association for Regional Cooperation (SAARC) region go to Sri Lanka. Of India's Sri Lanka-destined FDI, 63 per cent is in the services sector. Specific industries include health, education, hotel industry, tourism, IT training, computer software, and professional services.[76]

Another important economic link is tourism. Sri Lanka posted a 46 per cent upsurge in tourist arrivals following the end of civil war in 2009. India provided the largest number of tourists, overtaking the U.K., Germany, Maldives, and Australia.[77] India has also emerged as the preferred higher education and medical treatment destination for Sri Lankan citizens.

A recent World Bank report underscored India's importance to South Asian economic growth. The report stated, "The regional economic slowdown in 2011 mainly reflects a fall-off in activity in India, which represents about 80 per cent of South Asia's GDP, where growth is projected to ease to 8 per cent in FY2011/2012 from 8.8 per cent in FY 2010/11."[78]

[75]Central Bank of Sri Lanka, available at http://www.cbsl.gov.lk/

[76]Group of Fifteen, *News Bulletin*, May 2009, available at http://www.g15.org /bulletinmay09.pdf.

[77]The World Bank, available at http://web.worldbank.org

[78]Global Economic Prospects June 2011, Regional Annex, The World Bank, available at http://siteresources.worldbank.org/INTPROSPECTS/Resources/334934-1322593305595/8287139-1322766635825/GEP2011bSAR_Annex.pdf.

India's economic growth plays a crucial role in Sri Lanka's economic prospects. However, India has been unable to leverage this dependence. With the end of Sri Lanka's civil war, new investment opportunities have opened for Indian business houses. They view Sri Lanka as a fast growing economy with enormous potential for foreign investments, particularly its untapped Northern and Eastern Province markets. Such strong commercial interests have made it extremely difficult for India to leverage economic ties in order to achieve political objectives.[79] Intensifying pressure on the Sri Lankan leadership to address the war atrocities as well as resolving the Tamil issue, including through the devolution process, could create resentment within the Sri Lankan leadership. This in turn can result in lack of enthusiasm in Sri Lanka about Indian participation on the economic front.

Given its growing Chinese and Iranian ties, Colombo relies less on India, further limiting the latter's regional influence.[80] To India, the emerging situation is of no minimal geopolitical consequence.

THE ECONOMIC INTERDEPENDENCE OF SRI LANKA AND SAARC

The South Asia Free Trade Area (SAFTA), created under the auspices of the SAARC, plays a crucial role in Sri Lanka's economy. Figures from SAARC website illustrate that exports under SAFTA have grown considerably since the launching of the Trade Liberalisation Programme (TLP) in 2006 (See Table 6).[81]

[79]India and Sri Lanka after the LTTE, Asia Report, Available at http://www.crisisgroup.org.

[80]"China and conflict affected states," Safeworld, Available at http://www.saferworld.org.uk.

[81]SAARC website, South Asia Free Trade Area, Available at http://www.saarc-sec.org/areaofcooperation/detail.php?activity_id=5.

Table 6: Value of Exports Within SAFTA Member States (U.S.$)

Year	Bangladesh	India	Maldives	Pakistan	Sri Lanka	Total
2006	0	0	14,001.15	55,324.00	0	69,325.15
2007	15,273,177.84	3,783,410.31	0	576,164.99	19,828.02	19,652,581.16
2008	98,316,963.16	8,984,420.68	0	31,796,718.51	40,789.22	139,138,891.57
2009	199,786,454.72	315,256,736.34	0	43,509,984.90	608,623.96	559,161,799.92
2010	236,711,501.24	369,671,052.80	0	56,119,007.59	517,566.00	663,019,127.63
2011		287,810,462.38		43,174,978.83	102,393.00	331,087,834.21
2012		342,980,545.04				342,980,545.04
Total	550,088,096.96	1,328,486,627.55	14,001.15	175,232,178.82	1,289,200.20	2,055,110,104.68

Note: As indicated above, the figure of total cumulative value of exports under SAFTA has crossed U.S. $2 billion but it is far below the potential. For smooth functioning of the SAFTA, customs notifications for implementing Trade Liberalisation Programme (TLP) are issued as per the agreed timeline by the Member States. While reduction in the size of Sensitive Lists is important to increase the quantum of regional trade, efforts are being made to take out those products out of the Sensitive Lists that are of export interests to the SAARC Member States for trade within South Asia.

Source: SAARC official website, available at http://saarc-sec.org/areaofcooperation/detail.php?activity_id=5, Accessed on: 2 July, 2013.

Nevertheless, Sri Lanka's SAARC trade statistics do not paint an overly pleasing picture. From 2006-2010, Sri Lanka's exports to SAARC member states totalled U.S.$ 1,186,807.20. During the same period, Sri Lanka's imports from SAARC member states amounted to U.S. $1,471,784.47.[82]

Sri Lanka's SAARC trade has been quite low. The primary culprit is the large 'sensitive' list maintained by SAARC members.[83] Today, most tradable items are on the negative list of respective member states. Additionally, even with concessions granted under the South Asia Preferential Trade Agreement (SAPTA), most tradable items have been brought under the sensitive lists in SAFTA.

A reduction in the size of sensitive lists is important to increase trade volume between Sri Lanka and SAARC members. Additionally, efforts are being made to remove those products from sensitive lists that are of export interest to these states for intra-South Asia trade.

LEARNING FROM TRENDS—TRADE AND PROVINCES

In terms of trade, the North Central Province makes for a most interesting case study. Men constitute a majority of the employed population within Sri Lanka. The North Central Province has the highest male-to-female ratio (Appendix 1). This fact helps account for why the province has the second lowest level of poverty.[84] However, provincial literacy rates and pupil numbers continue to lag. The low female population has also contributed to a declining

[82]Department of Commerce, Government of Sri Lanka, *Export Achievements* 2011 available at http://www.doc.gov.lk/web/pdf/export_achievement_2011.pdf

[83]Items in a sensitive list (also known as negative list) are not offered concessional tariffs. Therefore, it is a list with every country which does not include the tariff concessions.

[84]Department of Census and Statistics, Government of Sri Lanka, *Household Income and Expenditure Survey*, available at http://www.statistics.gov.lk/HIES/HIES2009_10FinalReport.pdf.

young population. While this is currently beneficial to the province (as depicted by high household incomes), demographic trends make the future somewhat bleaker.

Certain factors must be considered if Sri Lanka intends to promote economic growth:

(1) Countering labour force contraction: Sri Lanka is witnessing both an increase in the unemployed female population and an increase in overall life expectancy. The country's labour force is on the decline, but there is huge pressure to provide for pension payments, old-age healthcare, and other issues that are typically 'aging' issues. This will be a significant burden on the country's economically active population and a constant pressure to maintain rapid GDP growth.

    Sri Lanka's labour force faces the danger of shrinking by 2030. As a primary production input, labour supply decline presents a massive challenge for this still-developing country.[85] The Sri Lankan government has tried to address these issues with a few specific policy measures. In 2011, it lifted the retirement age for public sector workers from 55 to 57, still low relative to other nations with a similar life expectancy. Additionally, the government attempted to legislate a new pension scheme bill in 2011. However, this project has been put on hold due to labour union protests.

(2) Female employment: With its proportion of women increasing, the Sri Lankan government seeks to promote female employment in the local economy. Steps taken by the government in this regard would go a long way in addressing some of the concerns of ethnic reconciliation as well, due to the fact that a substantial number of women are war widows in the war-affected areas. This is also in recognition of the fact

[85]World Bank, *Population Aging and the Labour Market: The Case of Sri Lanka*, available at http://siteresources.worldbank.org/SOCIALPROTECTION/Resources/SP-Discussion-papers/Labor-Market-DP/0821.pdf.

that female population has outnumbered the male population in most of the provinces. The need to address this issue has become all the more pressing. With low employment opportunities within Sri Lanka, many women are seeking overseas employment. Steps have already been taken by the government to reverse this trend by way of the National Labour Migration Policy (2008). While the policy is aimed at promoting opportunities for both men and women, it contains a special focus on women in order to stem the tide of women looking abroad for work.[86]

(3) Holistic development: From 2001-2010, Uva witnessed improvement in almost all social indicators considered. However, access to basic development resources continues to be limited. If the government wishes to achieve more integrated development, it must help provinces like Uva develop through focussed infrastructure development.

(4) Improve conditions in the Northern and Eastern Provinces: Lagging social indicators—including literacy, poverty, and household income—in the Eastern and Northern Provinces can be attributed to the Eelam War. Now that the war is over, there is a clear need for the government to step in, bringing about speedy socio-economic recovery within these provinces.

(5) Diversify export commodities: With high dependence on cloth exports, Sri Lanka faces a pressing need to diversify its export structure. The country should focus on developing an adequate market for its fastest growing sector, i.e., services.

(6) Modernise the agricultural sector: A large portion of Sri Lanka's population continues to depend on agriculture for livelihood. *Mahinda Chintana* inculcates efforts to address

[86]Ministry for Foreign Employment, Promotion and Welfare, International Labour Office, Colombo, *National Labour Migration Policy for Sri Lanka*, available at http://www.ilo.org/public/english/protection/migrant/download/mpolicy_srilanka_en.pdf.

this problem. Highlighting the need for an agricultural renaissance, the government has officially declared its responsibility to resolve the challenges faced by this sector.

(7) Investment: Although Sri Lanka's Board of Investment has managed to promote FDI inflows, mainly in services, the agricultural sector requires more investments. This is particularly true after the 2011 floods, which damaged a significant share of that year's early crop.

(8) India: While India remains apprehensive about increasing Chinese influence in the Indian Ocean Region, the country must realise that geography gives it an important advantage. India must leverage its proximity to Sri Lanka in order to deepen direct economic engagement.

VI

Role of External Powers

INTRODUCTION

Given its geostrategic location, Sri Lanka has dealt with external involvement since the 17th century, when a succession of Portuguese, Dutch, French, and British involved themselves in the island's affairs. The role of external powers has undergone dramatic changes in the past two decades—reflecting both fast-changing regional geopolitics and changes in the country's foreign policy orientation driven by internal needs. This chapter attempts to examine the role of external powers in Sri Lanka, analysing recent trends and likely directions in the coming years. In the recent past, there has been a growing trend of convergence between external factors and Colombo's internal compulsions and requirements. China, along with Pakistan to a lesser extent, is a case in point.

SRI LANKA-CHINA TIES

Although Sri Lanka-China relations stretch back decades, only in recent years have ties between Beijing and Colombo expanded and deepened.[87] In the face of growing Western criticism and cooling relations due to human rights issues, Colombo looked to China for

[87]See Nilanthi Samaranayake, "Are Sri Lanka's Relations with China Deepening? An Analysis of Economic, Military, and Diplomatic Data," *Asian Security*, vol. 7, no. 2, 2011, pp. 119–146; Thomas Wheeler, "China and Conflict-affected States between Principle and Pragmatism: Sri Lanka Case Study," *Saferworld*, January 2012.

diplomatic, economic, and military assistance. These factors have been driving the relationship. When the West criticised the Sri Lankan government for its handling of the ethnic conflict, Beijing provided political and strategic support that countered Western pressure. China and Russia consistently blocked resolutions aimed against Sri Lanka in various international fora, such as the U.N. Security Council.[88]

Another important geopolitical imperative relates to India. Just like any small-sized nation, Sri Lanka has tried to counterbalance India's influence by deepening ties with its main geopolitical rival, China.[89] Beijing wants to nose into what has been traditionally considered as India's backyard (i.e. the IOR), especially as the rivalry between the two Asian giants intensifies.[90] This strategy is not wholly dissimilar from India's attempts to gain influence in Southeast Asia and the South China Sea. Although Colombo has not overtly played India and China against each other, growing bonhomie between China and Sri Lanka cannot be ignored by India.[91]

Economic factors are also driving the Sri Lanka-China relationship. China's unconditional financial support to Sri Lanka

[88]In March 2009, China kept Sri Lanka off the agenda in the U.N. and then in May the same year, China along with Russia, India, and others defeated a European-backed resolution of the U.N. Human Rights Council (UNHRC) that tried to launch a war-crimes probe into the Sri Lankan government's actions.

[89]For instance, see "India and Sri Lanka after the LTTE," *Asia Report*, International Crisis Group, No. 206, June 23, 2011.

[90]For a discussion on China-India rivalry and the role of Sri Lanka, see Chietigj Bajpaee, "China-India Relations: Regional Rivalry Takes the World Stage," *China Security*, Vol. 6, No. 2, 2010, pp. 3–20; J. Mohan Malik, "South Asia in China's Foreign Relations," *Pacific Review*, Volume 13, Number 1, February 2001.

Willem van Kemenade, "Détente Between China and India: The Delicate Balance of Geopolitics in Asia," *Clingendael Diplomacy Papers*, Netherlands Institute of International Relations, No. 16, July 2008.

[91]Sudha Ramachandran, "India leery of Neighbor's New Squeeze," *Asia Times* online, August 16, 2011, available at http://www.atimes.com/atimes/south_asia/mh16df02.html.

provides Colombo much-needed financial support at a time when Western countries have conditioned aid donations. However, it must be noted that E.U. aid has continued uninterrupted with the exception of special aid packages provided to countries that uphold democratic values and human rights. China has also become a key trading partner of Sri Lanka, with bilateral trade reaching U.S. $2.78 billion in 2012.[92] In recent years, China has rapidly expanded development aid to Sri Lanka. In 2010, it emerged as the country's biggest financial donor, accounting for roughly U.S. $1.5 billion development aid. This number surpassed traditional major donors like Japan, Europe, and the U.S.[93]

China has also been involved in several significant infrastructure projects. These include the Hambantota port on Sri Lanka's south-eastern coast, expansion of the Colombo Port, renovation of the Bandaranaike International Conference Hall, and building an international airport at Mattala in Hambantota District. These projects cost roughly U.S. $190 million.[94] China also offered assistance in the implementation, improvement, design or construction of the following:

- Colombo-Katunayake Expressway
- Sri Lanka's railway network
- Coal power plant in Norochcholai
- Flood protection system for the suburbs of Colombo
- National Theatre for Performing Arts in Colombo

[92]Central Bank of China, *Annual Report 2012*, available at http://www.cbsl.gov.lk/pics_n_docs/10_pub/_docs/efr/annual_report/AR2012/English/17_Appendix.pdf.

[93]Chinese Media Reported Citing Sri Lankan Government Data. *People's Daily Online*, July 28, 2011, available at http://english.peopledaily.com.cn/90001/90776/90883/7453710.html.

[94]According to a recent media report, the country's second international airport at Mattala will be opened at the end of 2012. See *Colombo Page*, January 20, 2012, available at http://www.colombopage.com/archive_12/Jan20_1327079706CH.php.

- Special economic zone in Mirigama
- Rehabilitation of the Internally Displaced Persons (IDPs)
- Technical assistance for demining operations in the North and the East
- Rebuilding part of the railway line connecting Vavuniya with Jaffna[95]

In 2011, Sri Lanka sold one of its highest valued properties to the state-owned China Aviation Technology Import-Export Corporation (CATIC), which exports military aircraft to Sri Lanka. In the agreement, the land was earmarked for the construction of a luxury hotel. However, UNP (the main opposition party) raised strong objections regarding the desirability of selling "the best property in Sri Lanka" to a military hardware manufacturer that owned only a few hotels in China. Furthermore, the deal was sanctioned without a public tender, leading to more criticism of the government. Basil Rajapaksa, Economic Development Minister and brother of the Sri Lankan President, played a crucial role in securing cabinet approval for the deal.[96] The Rajapaksa regime first tried to salvage the deal through talks, but eventually the deal was scuttled amid mounting pressure. This case presented telling indications about Chinese business influence among the upper echelons of Sri Lanka's ruling elite. Additionally, and of equal significance, are the exposed rifts within the Sinhala polity.

China's economic boom and the likely growth of its south-western provinces will push China toward enhanced economic ties with South Asian nations, including Sri Lanka. China will continue to gain economically by further strengthening its foothold in Sri Lanka, which it sees as a 'priceless pearl' (in an IOR

[95]For more details on China-Sri Lanka's economic ties, see Nilanthi Samaranayake, "Are Sri Lanka's Relations with China Deepening? An Analysis of Economic, Military, and Diplomatic Data," *Asian Security*, vol. 7, no. 2, 2011, pp. 119–146.

[96]"Sri Lanka and China: About Face," *The Economist* (Colombo), October 29, 2012, available at http://www.economist.com/blogs/banyan/2011/10/sri-lanka-and-china.

'String of Pearls' strategy). The Hambantota Port could be used to protect China's SLOCs, and it has the potential to become a major hub and support base for China's Navy.

Sri Lanka's military success over the Tamil Tigers, ending the three decade-old civil war in 2009, benefited immensely from Chinese arms supplies. In the past few years, China has become Sri Lanka's largest supplier of weapons.[97] However, because much of Chinese aid comes in the form of market loans, payment obligations could strain Sri Lanka's economy.[98] Sri Lanka's defence budget in the post-war period increased, and a significant amount may be required to reimburse weapon costs built up during Eelam War IV.[99]

Despite growing economic, military, and diplomatic ties between Beijing and Colombo, there is little public information available revealing China's strategic designs for Sri Lanka.[100] However, if one analyses China's involvement in the broader

[97]For details, see Thomas Wheeler, "China and Conflict-affected States between Principle and Pragmatism: Sri Lanka Case Study," *Saferworld*, January 2012.

[98]During the war, the repayment arrangement worked with China because Sri Lanka could get military supplies from the Chinese firm, Norinco as and when there was a demand.

[99]The country has increased defence spending by about 7 per cent to U.S. $1.9 billion in 2011. See "Post-war Sri Lanka buys 14 military choppers from Russia," *Reuters*, August 17, 2011, available at http://in.reuters.com/article/2011/08/17/idINIndia-58832720110817; Saman Gunadasa, "Sri Lankan Government boosts military spending," *World Socialist* website, November 02, 2011, available at http://www.wsws.org/articles/2011/nov2011/slec-n02.shtml.

[100]In 2005, the Chinese government had conducted a study regarding its relations with countries in South Asia. The recommendations of the study included China to undertake measures to keep the current strategic leverage in terms of territory, P-5 membership, and the Nuclear Club, hold on to diplomatic advantages through its special relationship particularly with India's neighbouring countries, and also maintain the economic lead over India. The study, undertaken on the behest of Chinese leadership's "Foreign Affairs Cell," had incorporated inputs from China's South Asia specialists like Cheng Ruisheng, Ma Jiali, Sun Shihai, among others. See Mohan Malik, "Mohan Malik, "India-China Competition Revealed in Ongoing Border Disputes," *PINR Report*, October 09, 2007, available at http://www.pinr.com/report.php?ac= view_printable&report_id=695&language_id=1.

regional context, several factors would suggest that China's current commercial interests with Indian Ocean littorals dovetail well with future strategic priorities. Some see China's South Asia policy as "part of a carefully crafted long-term strategy that visualises it playing a leadership role" in the region.[101] Others argue that "China's interest in infrastructure development along the Indian Ocean coastline appears to be largely commercial."[102] While views differ regarding Chinese strategic aims in Sri Lanka, an analysis of its involvement in the Bay of Bengal region suggests that Beijing's commercial and strategic interests are likely to grow in the coming years. The major Chinese infrastructural projects in Sri Lanka, particularly the Hambantota Port and Mattala airport, will provide huge benefits to China and fit well within a larger strategy of regional connectivity. These projects will link to massive infrastructure projects that China has been developing in Myanmar and Bangladesh, which include railways, roads, pipelines, and seaports. [103]

The Bay of Bengal region projects (including deepwater ports) will allow for the use of mega-ships, so it is only natural that China would seek to use them as outlets both for its goods and to increase its IOR presence, a presence aimed at protecting crucial oil shipments.[104] While China's current IOR interests are primarily

[101]See for example, Parama Sinha Palit, "China's Soft Power in South Asia," *RSIS Working Paper*, No. 200, June 08, 2010, p. 22.

[102]See for instance, Nilanthi Samaranayake, "Are Sri Lanka's Relations with China Deepening? An Analysis of Economic, Military, and Diplomatic Data," *Asian Security*, vol. 7, no. 2, 2011, p. 140.

[103]For a discussion on China's involvement in Myanmar, see Hongwei Fan, "China's 'Look South': China-Myanmar Transport Corridor," *Ritsumeikan International Affairs*, Vol.10, 2011, pp.43–66.

[104]For example, commenting on the new Hambantota port being built by China, Sergei DeSilva-Ranasinghe, a Sri Lankan analyst, has argued that the port "will serve as a key transit point for oil and gas tankers accessing the Red Sea, Persian Gulf, Malacca Straits and the ports of Gwadar in Pakistan and Sittwe in Burma. Hambantota will also serve as a key maritime transit point to China's expanding investments among Indian Ocean island nations." See Sergei DeSilva-Ranasinghe, "Sri Lanka – The New Great Game," *Strategic Analysis Paper*, Future Directions International, March 24, 2010.

economic, the potential to gain strategic mileage in the future should not be overlooked. While there are purely commercial interests that drive China-Sri Lanka relationship, several long-run strategic imperatives may eventually supersede commercial interests. Recent writings by Chinese scholars provide some idea regarding China's strategic ambitions in the IOR. Hongwei Fan, a well-known Chinese scholar, argues that the "Sino-Myanmar transport corridor" will provide Beijing "an important measure of maintaining its influence and leading role in the arrangement of regional and sub-regional cooperation," and as a result will allow Chinese participation in Southeast Asia and South Asia cooperation. He further argues that the corridor will provide "the base" for China's "Two-Ocean strategy," referring to the Indian and Pacific Oceans.[105]

If Hongwei's views reflect Beijing's strategy in the IOR, an obvious question must be posed. Would Beijing convert Chinese-built ports in Sri Lanka, Pakistan, Myanmar, and Bangladesh into IOR naval bases in order to protect and promote regional strategic interests? According to some observers, there are signs that China is developing a "support network" for its navy in the IOR and that this trend is likely to "grow in the foreseeable future."[106]

However, most analysts currently believe that China will take years to convert the 'dependency/forward basing/logistical support' ports into military bases. Commenting on the subject, well-known scholars like Andrew S. Erickson and Gabriel Collins have argued that "China is currently far from having anything close to a naval base beyond Chinese waters."[107] They go on to note that for China "[t]o sustain a serious naval presence in the Indian Ocean, the PLAN would need to substantially expand its

[105]Hongwei Fan, "China's 'Look South': China-Myanmar Transport Corridor," *Ritsumeikan International Affairs*, Vol.10, 2011, pp. 56-60.

[106]See Daniel J. Kostecka, "The Chinese Navy's Emerging Support Network in the Indian Ocean," *China Brief*, The Jamestown Foundation, Volume X, Issue 15 July 22, 2010.

[107]Andrew S. Erickson and Gabriel Collins, "China's Maritime Evolution: Military and Commercial Factors," *Pacific Focus*, Vol. XXII, No. 2 (Fall 2007), p. 64.

at-sea replenishment capacity and also secure basing rights in locations such as Pakistan, Burma, and perhaps Sri Lanka or Bangladesh."[108] Scholar Daniel J. Kostecka has argued that to convert "these facilities into naval bases would require billions of dollars worth of military equipment and infrastructure in order to ensure their viability in wartime. Even then, the exposed position of these facilities makes their wartime utility dubious against an enemy equipped with long-range precision strike capability."[109] Even if Beijing desires naval bases in Sri Lanka or other IOR sites, the possibility of such a presence in the near future looks untenable. However, long-term possibilities cannot be ruled out, and New Delhi must keep a watchful eye on such developments.

Another argument also merits attention. There is a possibility that China may not convert civilian ports into full-fledged bases but merely utilise them as listening posts and signals intelligence stations, as it has done in at least one South China Sea island.

SRI LANKA AND THE WEST

Sri Lanka has had a traditionally pro-West orientation. However, in recent years relations with the West have spiralled downward. Since independence, the U.S. and Sri Lanka have traditionally had cordial relations. In 2007, Sri Lanka and the U.S. signed the Acquisition and Cross-Services Agreement (ACSA), which provided for logistics supplies and re-fuelling facilities for American ships and aircrafts and increased military inter-operability.[110] Therefore, U.S. armed forces have at least some small degree of military-to-military relations with the Sri Lankan

[108]Andrew S. Erickson and Gabriel Collins, "China's Maritime Evolution: Military and Commercial Factors," *Pacific Focus*, Vol. XXII, No. 2 (Fall 2007), p. 64.

[109]See Daniel J. Kostecka, "The Chinese Navy's Emerging Support Network in the Indian Ocean," *China Brief,* The Jamestown Foundation, Volume X, Issue 15, July 22, 2010.

[110]"Sri Lanka: Recharting U.S. Strategy after the War," Committee on Foreign Relations, United States Senate, 111th Congress, first session, December 07, 2009, available at http://www.foreign.senate.gov/imo/media/doc/SRI.pdf, p. 14.

defence establishment. The U.S. International Broadcast Bureau (IBB)—formerly the Voice of America (VOA)—also operates a radio-transmitting station in Sri Lanka. U.S. interest in Sri Lanka is interlinked with its interests in South Asia in particular and the Indian Ocean in general, mostly owing to Sri Lanka's geostrategic location. Sri Lanka is located at the crossroads of naval trading routes linking Europe and oil-rich West Asia to China and the rest of Asia. Thus, America's major regional interest revolves around ensuring the safety of Persian Gulf energy supplies headed for allies like Japan and ensuring the continued free flow of trade in the Indian Ocean.[111]

Terrorism, piracy, and interstate conflict/instability are other major regional concerns for the U.S. China's increased engagement with Sri Lanka has increased the country's strategic importance to the U.S. America remains Sri Lanka's most important single country export market, accounting for 21 per cent of total exports and over 40 per cent of garment exports in 2010.[112] However, the relationship currently has a downward trajectory. U.S. concerns about alleged human rights violations during the final stages of the Eelam War have hampered relations. Aid was a major component of U.S. involvement in Sri Lanka. In fact, U.S. aid increased from US$ 12.8 million in 2000 to US$ 82.3 million in 2009. Similarly, U.S. military assistance to Colombo also increased from US$ 0.3 million in 2000 to US$ 7.7 million in 2009. Total economic and military assistance to Sri Lanka in 2010 stood at US$ 109.52 million.[113] According to OECD data, in 2008–2009 the U.S. was Sri Lanka's second biggest country donor after Japan.

[111]"Sri Lanka: Recharting U.S. Strategy after the War," Committee on Foreign Relations, United States Senate, 111th Congress, first session, December 07, 2009, available at http://www.foreign.senate.gov/imo/media/doc/SRI.pdf, p.12.

[112]"U.S. State Department, Background Note: Sri Lanka," available at http://www.state.gov/r/pa/ei/bgn/5249.htm.

[113]U.S. AID Greenbook, available at http://gbk.eads.usaidallnet.gov/query/do.

With the conclusion of the war, the U.S. is seriously rethinking its aid to Sri Lanka. In July 2011, the House Foreign Affairs Committee unanimously banned all non-humanitarian aid over alleged war crimes by Sri Lankan forces during the Eelam War. This ban will remain in effect until the administration certifies that Colombo has shown progress on the human rights issue. However, a U.S. Senate report warned against allowing U.S.-Sri Lanka relations to deteriorate because of human rights, as this strategy will harm U.S. interests.[114] Though concern about human rights will continue to drive a wedge between Sri Lanka and the U.S., it is unlikely to completely dominate the long-term agenda. Given American strategic interests in Sri Lanka, especially when China's deepening engagement is considered, the U.S.-Sri Lanka relationship cannot stay hamstrung for too long. However, for the time being, the relations have hit an all-time low after the U.S. sponsored resolutions against Sri Lanka twice in a row at the U.N. Human Rights Council in Geneva.

E.U.-Sri Lanka relations are also far from cordial. As with the U.S., E.U.-Sri Lanka relations have suffered due to alleged human rights violations by Sri Lankan armed forces during the Eelam War. The E.U. has made several attempts to pass resolutions against Sri Lanka in the U.N. Security Council and U.N. Human Rights Council, but it was thwarted by Russia and China. Some E.U. countries halted aid to Sri Lanka, while others emphasized human rights in their aid programmes. In July 2010, the E.U. withdrew Sri Lanka's access to the Generalised System of Preferences Plus (GSP+) over human rights concerns. Despite these moves, the E.U. remains Sri Lanka's biggest export market and a major donor, particularly in post-war recovery projects.

Human rights concerns are likely to continue dominating Sri Lanka-E.U. relations as the E.U. lacks a major strategic interest in

[114]"Sri Lanka: Recharting U.S. Strategy after the War," Committee on Foreign Relations, United States Senate, 111th Congress, first session, December 07, 2009, available at http://www.foreign.senate.gov/imo/media/doc/SRI.pdf, p.16.

Sri Lanka. However, it is against Sri Lanka's interests to completely antagonise the West and rely exclusively on China. Sri Lanka needs Western assistance in tackling the economically strong Diaspora, who could potentially revive the ethnic issue. The strength of the Sri Lankan Tamil Diaspora is estimated to be 1.2 million living in Europe and North America.[115] As of now, Sri Lanka's economy continues to be heavily dependent on exports to the West, a trend likely to continue. Given that exports are a major driver of Sri Lanka's economy, relations with Western nations must be attended to assiduously.

SRI LANKA-PAKISTAN TIES

Pakistan-Sri Lanka relations have deepened in the recent past. India is a key driver of the relationship. While Pakistan views India as the regional hegemon, Sri Lanka too has concerns about the big brother in its neighbourhood. On the one hand, Colombo has sought to increase its strategic choices by engaging Islamabad in recent years, but on the other, Pakistan sees its enhanced ties with Sri Lanka as a natural occurrence. A highlight of the growing Colombo-Islamabad relationship is their military ties, evident from enormous arms sales during the Eelam War years. The relationship has been further bolstered with regular high-level bilateral visits and exchanges. Most recently, Pakistan's Chief of Army Staff, General Ashfaq Kayani, was in Sri Lanka to address the passing out parade ceremony at Sri Lankan Military Academy. During the visit, General Kayani emphasised Pakistan's renewed military commitment to Sri Lanka and agreed to strengthen dialogue on defence and security

[115]"Leon Berenger, Govt. Moves to Silence Tamil Diaspora Threat," *The Sunday Times,* May 31, 2009, available at http://www.sundaytimes.lk/090531/News/sundaytimesnews_14.html (accessed on June 23, 2012).

matters.[116] Defence production was particularly highlighted in this context.[117]

Islamabad has long tried to move Colombo from New Delhi's side through supplying weapons. Pakistan has emerged as a key weapons supplier to Sri Lanka and has also provided training to Sri Lankan soldiers. Pakistan positioned itself to play a key role in Sri Lanka's post-war reconstruction efforts. Observers believe that Islamabad's interest is a consequence of deepening China-Sri Lanka ties. Pakistan feels it can piggy-back on China's growing influence, furthering economic ties with Colombo and tamping down India's regional ambitions. However, one potential area of discord between Sri Lanka and Pakistan relates to exports, a major economic driver for both nations. Intense competition over Western garment export markets may introduce rivalries and tensions into the Pakistan-Sri Lanka relationship.

Meanwhile, several reports indicate that Pakistan is getting involved in Sri Lanka's East, contributing to growing radicalisation of the Muslim community. This could emerge as a major security threat and complicate ties with Pakistan. An Indian newspaper quoted B. Raman, former Additional Secretary in the Cabinet Secretariat, who noted that some Pakistani diplomats in Colombo sent Sri Lankan Muslims to the radical Binori madrasa in Karachi, where they received scholarships for religious

[116]A few instances of the growing Sri Lanka-Pakistan partnership include: visit by the Foreign Secretary of Pakistan, Mr. Jalil Abbas Jilani, to Sri Lanka in April 2013; six-day visit by a four-member Pakistan Navy delegation in February 2013; visit to Pakistan by the Commander of the Sri Lankan Navy Vice Admiral Jayanth Colombage in November 2012; Pakistan's Naval Ship, *Azmat*, a missile fitted Fast Attack Craft FAC (M), was visiting Sri Lanka from May 28-31, 2012 on her maiden voyage to Pakistan after its commissioning in China. For details, see Press Section, Pakistan High Commission in Sri Lanka, available at http://www.pakistanhc.lk/category/news/.

[117]Press Section, Pakistan High Commission in Sri Lanka, "Pakistan, Sri Lanka for closer cooperation in defence production," September 06, 2012, available at http://www.pakistanhc.lk/2012/09/pakistan%E2%80%9A-sri-lanka-for-closer-cooperation-in-defence-production/.

education arranged by the Tablighi Jamat.[118] More recently, Wikileaks cables revealed that the Pakistan-based terror outfit, Lashkar-e-Tayyeba (LeT), had established a 'support centre' in Sri Lanka, which Colombo has denied.[119] Colombo apparently has grave concerns about the spread of Pakistan-linked terrorism, which they fear will redound on Sri Lankan and Indian targets. As of now, no concrete evidence suggests ISI involvement in the radicalisation of Sri Lankan Muslims.

Saudi Arabia, meanwhile, is reported to be funding Wahhabism in Sri Lanka by supporting madrasas, mosques and the training of preachers.[120] According to Riyyaz M. Sally, President of the Islamic Solidarity Front, "scholarships are given to young Lankan Muslims to go to religious institutions in Saudi Arabia. They are sent back to spread Wahhabism."[121] While there exists no concrete evidence to demonstrate that Sri Lanka has been targeted by Saudi Arabia, Wahhabism has become more popular than the traditional moderate form of Islam practised in Sri Lanka, particularly in its Eastern province.[122] Under the influence of Wahhabism, Sri Lankan Islam has transformed from the 1970s and early 1980s. Several clashes between Wahhabists and non-Wahhabists have been reported in the Eastern Province,

[118]Quoted in A.R.M. Imtiyaz, "The Eastern Muslims of Sri Lanka: Special Problems and Solutions," *Journal of Asian and African Studies*, Vol. 44 (4), August 2009, p. 420.

[119]Santhush Fernando, "Sri Lanka: U.S. cable reveals foreign terror group in Lanka-Wikileaks," December 08, 2012, *Asian Tribune*, available at http://www.asiantribune.com/news/2010/12/08/sri-lanka-us-cable-reveals-foreign-terror-group-lanka-wikileaks.

[120]Though there are no concrete figures to show the amount of funds to Sri Lanka, it is understood that the Saudis are spending billions of dollars annually across the globe for spreading Wahhabism.

[121]"Saudi Petro Dollars Behind Growing Islamic Extremism in Sri Lanka." *The New Indian Express*, September 20, 2010, available at http://www.thememriblog.org/urdupashtu/blog_personal/en/30532.htm.

[122]"Militant Wahabism beats other Islamic fundamentalists in Sri Lanka," August 28, 2007, *Asian Tribune*, available at http://www.asiantribune.com/index.php?q=node/7156.

while shrines of Sufi saints have been demolished in the name of 'Islamic purification.'[123] Clearly, radicalisation is growing among a section of the country's Muslim population. The Sri Lankan government is acutely aware of the dangers posed by radicalisation. In fact, Sri Lanka evicted some foreign Muslim clerics (including those from India, Pakistan, Maldives, and some Arab countries) in early 2012.[124]

Colombo is particularly concerned about the influence of Islamic radicalisation emanating from neighbouring Maldives. Although no evidence currently exists to support this fear, increasing religious conservatism in Maldives is a cause for worry in the future. Because extremists have taken to modern communication tools with ease, geographic and political boundaries no longer form a barrier to radicalisation. These 'virtual' challenges pose a threat to Sri Lanka and the region at large. It is imperative that India remains vigilant and cooperates closely with Sri Lanka and other neighbours to deal with this problem.

SRI LANKA AND OTHER MAJOR PLAYERS

Sri Lanka-Russia ties are increasingly cordial, even as relations with the West decline. Although Russian interests in Sri Lanka may be limited, they are fairly multi-faceted. Russia has consistently backed Sri Lanka in international fora, particularly during and after the Eelam War. The state-run Russian oil firm Gazprom has been in talks with Sri Lanka about exploring oil and gas off the coast of Mannar (to Sri Lanka's east) and also agreed to supply oil at concessionary rates. Colombo's economic interests in Moscow will continue to grow because Russia offers a huge market

[123]Dennis B. Mcgilvray and Mirak Raheem, "Muslim Perspectives on the Sri Lankan Conflict," *Policy Studies* 41, 2007, East West Center, available at http://www.eastwestcenter.org/sites/default/files/private/ps041.pdf, p.43.

[124]"Sri Lanka 'expels 161 foreign Muslim preachers,'" *BBC News,* January 22, 2012, available at http://www.bbc.co.uk/news/world-asia-16675086.

for tea. Russia is also a major supplier of arms. In 2010, both countries signed a U.S. $300 million line of credit for the sale of armaments and dual-purpose technology to Sri Lanka.[125] Russia sees its relations with Sri Lanka as giving it a foothold in the IOR.

Iran is another external player gradually strengthening its ties with Sri Lanka. It originally became involved with Sri Lanka through soft loans and infrastructure investments. Iran's role in Sri Lanka's energy matrix is also important, as Iran is a principle supplier of Sri Lanka's crude oil needs. In fact, Sri Lanka's only refinery—Sapugaskanda—can only process Iranian crude.[126] In 2011, 93 per cent of Sri Lanka's crude oil imports were from Iran.[127] Furthermore, during the Eelam war, Iran provided oil to Colombo at special concessionary rates and gave low-interest loans for buying Chinese and Pakistani defence equipment. Some believe Iran is also cooperating with China to build deep water ports in Sri Lanka, as part of a joint strategy of ensuring the uninterrupted flow of oil and gas from Iran to China and technology from China to Iran.[128] Iran has also invested in energy-related projects, particularly oil refineries, not only for Sri Lanka's domestic consumption but also aimed at export to China.[129] In return, Sri Lanka has publicly supported Iran's right to pursue nuclear energy options.

[125] Shyam Tekwan, "Sri Lanka: Transnational Security and Post-insurgency Issues," 2012, Asia Pacific Centre for Security Studies, available at http://www.apcss.org/wp-content/uploads/2012/02/154-166-Sri-Lanka.pdf, p.159.

[126] Shamindra Ferdinando, "U.S. Action against Iran Affects SL Post-War Recovery," February 01, 2012, *The Island*, available at http://www.island.lk/index.php?page_cat=article-details&page=article-details&code_title=44449.

[127] R.K. Radhakrishnan, "Anxieties over Oil Grows in Sri Lanka," *The Hindu*, February 06, 2012.

[128] Jamsheed K. Choksy, "Why Iran's Blue-Water Naval Ambition Matters," August 05, 2011, *The American Interest*, available at http://www.the-american-interest.com/article.cfm?piece=1025.

[129] Jamsheed K. Choksy, "A Sino-Persian Grab for the Indian Ocean?," *Small Wars Foundation*, July 07, 2011, available at http://smallwarsjournal.com/blog/journal/docs-temp/810-choksy.pdf,p.3.

Sri Lanka has other important partners in West Asia. The U.A.E., for instance, provides Sri Lanka's largest Persian Gulf export market and third largest source of FDI. Sri Lanka imports crude oil, gas, and lubricants from the U.A.E., which is also a major importer of Sri Lankan tea. Through the OPEC fund, the U.A.E. and Saudi Arabia are also emerging as major players in Sri Lanka's development projects.

Israel has also continued to be a player in Sri Lanka's West Asia equations mainly as a supplier of military technology and equipment. Israel also reportedly trained Sri Lankan pilots and assisted in its war against the LTTE.

Japan remains a major donor, accounting for nearly 30 per cent of Sri Lanka's 2011 aid. Japan, like India, would like to stave off a too-close Sri Lanka-China relationship, given that essential oil supplies pass through SLOCs adjacent to Sri Lanka. Some Japanese firms have also expressed interest in exploring Mannar Basin oil.

Meanwhile, like Japan, Australia also is a major donor to Sri Lanka. Unlike many Western nations, they have not come down heavily on the human rights issue. Australia will likely maintain a more nuanced policy towards Sri Lanka for two reasons. First, it hosts a large proportion of the Sri Lankan Diaspora. Second, Australia sees Sri Lanka's geostrategic location in the IOR as holding immense value. Additionally, Australia sees the potential for major investments in Sri Lanka's mining industry, given its huge mineral reserves—such as phosphate, graphite, and Mannar Basin gas.

Thus far, Colombo seems to have succeeded in reaping defence and commercial benefits by playing geostrategic rivals off one another, notably with China/Pakistan and India. However, adequately addressing the human rights question could mean even greater support from and engagement with the U.S. and E.U. nations. Whether this time-tested counter-balancing strategy will change or remain as effective in the future remains an open question. So long as Colombo's strategy succeeds, it works in favour of the country, although there could be concerns for India. At the worst, if Sri Lanka's current threading of the proverbial needle fails and if the balancing strategy provokes a major power confrontation over Sri Lanka, the results could be politically and economically harmful. Additionally, India must be ever-mindful of Sri Lanka inadvertently coming too much under the influence of any one power with interests perceived as inimical to India's own. Sri Lanka's relations vis-à-vis foreign powers is currently benefitting most parties involved, but there is little reason to believe that geopolitical rivalries playing out in the IOR could not contribute to this status quo shifting in a more negative direction moving forward.

VII

India-Sri Lanka Relations: Present and Future Trends

Introduction

Historically, India and Sri Lanka have enjoyed close cultural, linguistic, and religious ties. However, in the post-independence era, several issues—including Indian Tamils and maritime disputes surrounding Kachchaitivu—made bilateral relations more tumultuous. Efforts by the two governments to find an amicable solution led to five key agreements: the Nehru-Kotelawala Agreement (1954); Indo-Ceylon (Sirimao-Shastri) Agreement (1964); Indira Gandhi-Bandaranaike Agreement (1974); Rajiv-Jayawardane Accord (1987); and the Indo-Sri Lanka Free Trade Agreement (1998).[130]

Tamil-Sinhalese ethnic strife, extreme persecution of minority Tamils, and domestic pressure from Tamil Nadu forced India to take measures that later constricted its Sri Lanka policy. Despite best intentions, New Delhi could not enforce its role as an acceptable moderator in the conflict. As the IPKF mission demonstrated, the attempt to play mediator between the Sri Lankan government and LTTE often strained the Indo-Sri Lankan diplomatic relationship, in addition to having human and economic costs.

The first two bilateral accords dealt with citizenship of Indian Tamils, although the issue was not fully resolved until the 1974

[130]Jayanta Kumar Ray, *India's Foreign Relations,* New Delhi, Routledge, 2011.

agreement. After the 1948 Citizenship Act rendered Indian Tamils stateless in Sri Lanka, an attempt to settle the issue was made by the Nehru-Kotewala agreement in 1954. The agreement suggested registration of stateless persons under the Indian and Pakistan Residents (Citizenship) Act of 1949, although this was not implemented. Finally, under the 1974 agreement, about 600,000 people were repatriated to India, while 514,000 remained in Sri Lanka.[131]

Bilateral relations were also punctuated by the maritime dispute over Kachchaitivu. The Sirimao-Shastri Agreement of 1964 had provisions whereby India agreed to Sri Lanka's sovereignty over Kachchaitivu with some safeguards for Indian fishermen.

Having resolved the two major outstanding bilateral issues by the early 1970s, relations remained cordial until the early 1980s. When the LTTE militancy began in 1983, bilateral relations deteriorated with the growth of Sri Lanka's suspicions and fear. Even as India played the dual role of mediating the conflict and coercing the involved parties, the Sri Lankan government perceived the Indian role to be biased and its interests particularly favouring the Tamils. The Indira Gandhi-led Indian government became suspicious of Sri Lankan motives once the UNP government sought military assistance from extra-regional powers. Sri Lanka's move on this front and U.S. involvement in the subcontinent prompted India to declare the 'Indira Doctrine,'[132] which discouraged the involvement of extra-regional players in India's neighbourhood.

Rajiv Gandhi's term in the mid-1980s saw an upswing in relations. Under his leadership, the 1987 India-Sri Lanka Accord was concluded.[133] The Accord acknowledged Sri Lanka as a multi-

[131]*ibid.*

[132]Devin T. Hagerty. "India's Regional Security Doctrine," *Asian Survey*, 1991, available at http://www.jstor.org/stable/10.2307/2645389.

[133]Shantha K. Hennayake, "The Peace Accord and the Tamils in Sri Lanka," *Asian Survey*, 1989.

ethnic, multilingual and multireligious society. It recognised that each ethnic group had a distinct cultural/linguistic identity and agreed that the Northern and Eastern Provinces were "areas of historical habitation of Tamil speaking peoples." The Accord also provided for the cessation of hostilities and disarmament of militants, as well as the return of Sri Lanka's Army to its barracks.

The Accord also codified the 13th Amendment, while the Provincial Councils Act was passed in the Sri Lankan Parliament in 1987. The amendment included key provisions for devolution of powers in the civil, police, and judicial domains, while also declaring Tamil as an official language of Sri Lanka alongside Sinhala. The following measures were also agreed upon:

- Merger of the Northern and Eastern Province (subject to an Eastern Province referendum);
- Appointment of provincial governors;
- Establishment of provincial-level high courts;
- Creation of central, provincial, and concurrent lists including subjects which could be made into laws.[134]

However, financial decisions were still to be made by the Parliament, with division of powers remaining somewhat opaque. The Centre was still to exercise unilateral control in many areas. The President retained the authority to overrule provincial acts under the Public Safety Ordinance, restricting provincial exclusivity with respect to any subject.

The 1987 Agreement laid down some vital principles with respect to Sri Lankan unity and sovereignty, sensitivity to Tamil aspirations, and ethnic strife vis-à-vis India's geostrategic

[134]In federalist systems, there are three lists concerning relations between centre and states—Central List, State List and Concurrent List. Central lists include those subjects on which the central government has complete administrative and legislative control; state list consists of those items wherein the state has total administrative and legislative control; and concurrent list consists of those items wherein both centre and states have responsibilities. However, in case of a clash, the centre will prevail.

interests. India agreed to deny Tamil separatists Indian bases or facilities and to provide naval assistance to counter the threat. Meanwhile, Sri Lanka agreed to consult India on the role of all external military and intelligence agencies and to review the use of foreign broadcasting units. Additionally, Sri Lanka agreed to deny Trincomalee Port for military use by any country in a way detrimental to Indian interests. Critically, the lack of formal LTTE acceptance of the Indo-Lankan Accord allowed the LTTE to reject its precepts and refused to surrender arms.

The decision to send in the IPKF as a mediator cost India dearly. Consequently, IPKF withdrawal, under pressure from the Premadasa-led Sri Lankan government, became a defining lesson in India's Sri Lanka policy and a reference point for future decisions on intervention. Even after Rajiv Gandhi was assassinated for Indian involvement in Sri Lanka, policy ambivalence on this front continued. Post-1991 saw an era of non-intervention and quiet diplomacy from the Indian side. India extended complete support to the Norwegian peace process. Testing the resilience of this approach, India withstood domestic political compulsions and facilitated the final defeat of the LTTE during the concluding phases of the Eelam War.

TAMIL AND THE TAMIL NADU FACTOR

Tamil Nadu politics has had a considerable impact on India's reaction to Sri Lanka's internal developments. In fact, Sri Lanka has emerged as a case study for the interaction of domestic politics and foreign policy. The concept of 'pan Tamil' identity emerged both from Tamil persecution in Sri Lanka and the prevailing political spirit of Tamil Nadu. Electoral politics were influenced increasingly by lingual identity (derived from caste consciousness) with a strong undertone of autonomous 'Dravidanadu' identity. In fact, this was the major electoral plank of the regional DMK Party, which came to power with the 1967 electoral defeat of the Congress Party.

The Nehruvian era witnessed a strong central government and a Congress-led state. Policy decisions, especially those impinging upon foreign and security affairs, were guided by the Nehruvian dictum of "non interference in internal affairs of other countries." After 1983, the eruption of the Tamil conflict, the large-scale inflow of refugees, and pressure from regional parties dictated a more direct Sri Lanka policy.[135] This is why Prime Minister Indira Gandhi categorically said to Jayawardane: "India cannot be regarded as just any country."[135a] India would be affected by domestic developments in Sri Lanka. Therefore, Sri Lanka must pay attention to its concerns. During this period, competitive Dravidian politics affected both parties. The Karunanidhi-led DMK and MG Ramachandran-led AIADMK tried to outdo each other in displaying solidarity with Sri Lankan Tamils and pressurising the centre. DMK took it one step further by boycotting a returning IPKF mission and openly criticising central government policy. DMK paid a heavy electoral price for this stand in 1991, following the Rajiv Gandhi assassination.

The assassination was a turning point for Tamil Nadu politics. Barring the miniscule electoral power-yielding MDMK chief Vaiko, who incidentally had to spend 18 months in jail under the Prevention of Terrorism Act (POTA) for supporting LTTE, the major parties made a clear distinction between their support for the Tamils and the violence perpetrated by LTTE. The entire political spectrum, led by Jayalalitha's AIADMK, distanced itself from the LTTE, with some even taking an altogether antagonistic stand. Tamil solidarity continued in different ways. The DMK agreed to host the Tamil National Alliance and facilitate talks with the centre. Jayalalitha refused to host President Rajapaksa on his maiden visit to India in December 2005. Even as AIADMK has distanced itself from LTTE, it has continued with its demand for international investigation of the war crimes, clearly an indicator that finding a solution to the ethnic conflict is still an important factor in Tamil Nadu politics.

[135]*ibid.*

[135a]Neil Devotta, "Is India Over-Extended? When Domestic Disorder Precludes Regional Intervention," *Contemporary South Asia,* Vol. 12, Issue 3, September 2003, pp. 365-380.

Over the years, the Tamil issue has lost its salience that existed in the 1980s and 1990s. However, the central government still lacks a free hand in crafting Sri Lanka policy; Tamil Nadu must always be considered. This was most recently evident at the March 2013 UNHRC (UN Human Rights Council) vote in Geneva.[136] Both the DMK (an important coalition ally of the UPA Government) and AIADMK (current Tamil Nadu State government) strongly advocated support for the resolution. Consequently, India did succumb to coalition compulsions although both the Tamil political parties felt that the final text of the resolution was a diluted one. This trend will likely continue, as regional political parties have continued clout with their coalition allies at the centre.

Post-LTTE, India has done a delicate balancing act on Sri Lanka relations. India has shown patience by not putting too much pressure on the Rajapaksa government to find a political solution to ethnic reconciliation. However, India remains unhappy that in the four years since concluding the war against the LTTE, no concrete steps have yet been taken by the Rajapaksa government.

In addition to the Tamil Nadu political factor, some in the Indian intelligentsia and strategic community now question India's Sri Lanka policy.[137] Many believe the Geneva vote was a pragmatic play. They are not apologetic. The Rajapaksa government's continuing ambivalence regarding dialogue with the TNA, 'tactical retreat' from the 13th amendment clause, and lack of movement on devolution triggered India's 'inclination' to vote for the resolution.

[136]India had voted against Sri Lanka in March 2012 also.

[137]Gulbin Sultana. "UNHRC Resolution on Sri Lanka: India's Options," Institute of Defence Studies and Analyses, March 23, 2012, available at http://www.idsa.in/idsacomments/UNHRCResolutiononSriLankaIndiasOptions_gsultana_190312; "A Wake Up Call for Colombo," *The Hindu*, March 23, 2012 available at http://www.thehindu.com/todays-paper/tp-opinion/article3156768.ece.

However, India's decision has been criticised for lacking strategic vision[138] and succumbing to coalition politics; in other words, unduly allowing domestic politics to dictate foreign policy and national security interests. Some suggested that India should have voted against, while also extracting concrete assurances regarding actions to be taken in Sri Lanka. The controversy once again highlighted the far-reaching impact of competitive Dravidian politics, which most studies have dismissed as having little electoral relevance.

However, the Geneva vote does not completely nullify this argument. India has been presented with an unprecedented combination of circumstances. Domestically, a weak coalition controls the central government. Internationally, this is a time of heightened sensitivity to human rights violations, given the situation in Syria. Coupled with Sri Lanka's glacial, opaque approach to devolution, these circumstances forced India's hand on the Geneva vote at this particular time.

New Delhi also remains concerned about potential spill-over effects from ethnic conflict, particularly a refugee influx into mainland and the political ramifications in Tamil Nadu and other Indian states. At the conflict's peak, there were as many as 20,000-30,000 refugees crossing over into India on a daily basis. The number has tapered off since the end of the war, but a significant number of refugees continue to live within India. Many of those who returned to Sri Lanka are unhappy with the poor economic conditions of the North and East provinces. There is little opportunity for employment, as even setting up cottage industries has proved difficult for the Tamils. People returning to agriculture and farming also docs not appear to be an option in the near future

[138]Rajesh Rajagopalan, "Human Rights and India's Foreign Policy," *Analysis*, Observer Research Foundation, March 26, 2012 available at http://orfonline.org/cms/sites/orfonline/modules/analysis/AnalysisDetail.html?cmaid=34936&mmacmaid=34937.

as most of the arable lands were burnt down in the final phase of the Eelam War.

Meanwhile, Sri Lankan Tamils in India are treated as de facto citizens, without being subjected to arbitrary detention or restriction on movement. In fact, they receive the same elementary education in Tamil Nadu schools and universities as Indian nationals. The state government has specially allocated slots for Sri Lankan Tamil students. The state government also provides them with cash assistance, food rations, and space to build a house, in addition to all social services available to Indians.

However, India remains concerned at the prospect of LTTE sleeper cells in Tamil Nadu (and possibly elsewhere). These could feed into nascent Tamil nationalist/separatist movements that may once again erupt in Sri Lanka.

The return of Tamil refugees has been a major aspect of Indo-Sri Lanka relations. The arrival of Sri Lankan Tamil refugees into Tamil Nadu happened in multiple waves:[139]

- First wave: Occurred in the aftermath of the 1983 riots over a four-year period leading up to the Indo-Sri Lankan Accord. An estimated 134,000 refugees came into India, and 25,585 returned after the signing of the accord.
- Second wave: Coincided with the second Eelam War (1990-1995), with nearly 122,000 refugees crossing into India. Following Rajiv Gandhi's assassination, the Jayalalitha regime in Tamil Nadu expedited the repatriation process, sending back over 50,000 refugees.
- Third wave: Coincided with the third Eelam War (1995-2002), when nearly 23,500 refugees came to India. The tide ebbed with the 2002 ceasefire agreement. The period 2002-2006 saw the return of about 10,000 refugees. According to United Nations High Commissioner for Refugees (UNHCR)

[139] V. Suryanarayan, "Sri Lanka: Focus on the Sri Lankan Tamil Refugees," South Asia Analysis Group, 2009, Web, March 23, 2012, available at http://http://www.southasiaanalysis.org/%5Cpapers36%5Cpaper3502.html.

figures, by the end of 2005, there were about 50,000 Sri Lankan refugees in India.[140]

- The number of refugees increased significantly during the final stages of the war. In fact, the last wave of refugees came in between 2006 and 2009.

India is not a party to the 1951 Refugee Convention or its 1967 Protocol.[141] Although it is a signatory to U.N. and World Convention on Human Rights, Refugee Issues and Related Matters, India has no refugee protection framework. The nation's stated policy is that refugees should repatriate when normalcy is returned. However, this must be read in consonance with the internationally accepted principle of 'non-refoulement'[142] of refugees to the country of their origin.

It is reported that there are around 140,000 Sri Lankan refugees across the globe, of which a majority is said to be in India. Around 70,000 people are said to be living in 112 refugee camps in Tamil Nadu and another 30,000 live outside camps in India.[143] Repatriation of refugees has been going on although it is believed to be at a slow pace. For instance, around 2,000 people are believed to have gone back in 2011, increasing from 823 in 2009. Most returnees settled in Trincomalee, Mannar, Vavuniya, and Jaffna.[144]

[140] *2005 UNHRC Statistical Yearbook*, available at http://www.unhcr.org/4641be59e.html

[141] Ananthachari, T., "Refugees in India: Legal Framework, Law Enforcement and Security," *ISIL Year Book of International Humanitarian and Refugee Law*, 2001, available at http://www.worldlii.org/int/journals/ISILYBIHRL/2001/7.html.

[142] This means they can be repatriated only with voluntary consent. This has been substantiated by repeated court judgements in cases like P. Nedumaran vs. Union of India, Mohammadi vs. Union of India, Maiwand's Trust of Afghan Human Freedom vs. State of Punjab, etc.

[143] Integrated Regional Information Networks (IRIN), "Sri Lanka: Tamil refugees slowly return from India," January 11, 2012, available at http://www.refworld.org/docid/4f0fed552.html.

[144] IRIN, "Sri Lanka: Tamil Refugees Slowly Return From India," *Eurasia Review*, January 12, 2012, available at http://www.eurasiareview.com/12012012-sri-lanka-tamil-refugees-slowly-return-from-india/.

Reasons cited for return include family unification, poor living conditions in refugee camps, and concerns over property left behind in Sri Lanka. Older refugees are more inclined to return than the younger ones.[145] According to UNHCR, basic problems in refugee return include slow demining, continued military occupation, lack of basic infrastructure, and employment/economic opportunities (lack of).

Even as the Sri Lankan government continues to give priority to the repatriation of Internally Displaced Peoples (IDPs), UNHCR asserts that the situation of IDPs and refugees is comparable, suggesting they should be given equal priority.

IMPACT OF SRI LANKA'S EXTERNAL RELATIONS ON INDIA

As an immediate neighbour with strong ethno-linguistic linkages, Sri Lanka's foreign relations are likely to have a greater impact on India than any other neighbour. Consequently, gauging Sri Lanka's relations with China will be a top priority for Indian strategic thinkers. Beijing has two clear advantages over India. First, its overt support and supply of arms during the LTTE war strongly reinforced Sri Lanka-China ties. China is Sri Lanka's biggest supplier of weapons. Second, after the war, China consistently blocked human rights-instigated resolutions aimed against Colombo in international arenas. India has suffered on both accounts.

Additionally, in terms of aid and developmental assistance, China continues to focus on southern Sri Lanka, which is unlike India. Also, China is participating in building the Vavuniya-Jaffna railway line. India must attempt to prevent the impression of a bifurcated Sri Lanka with an India-developed North and China-

[145]Cited examples include that of marriage, where having married within Indian Tamil society, resettling would be difficult. The other case is that of unmarried women, who are reluctant due to lower number of men of marriageable age among Sri Lankan Tamils, leading to high dowry demands.

developed South. This situation would position China and India on opposite sides of ethnic tensions.

India needs to make conscious and substantial efforts to match the efficiency of Chinese infrastructure construction, especially regarding time efficiency. An important area would be port infrastructure projects, as highlighted in previous chapters. However, given China's efficiency and India's inadequate resources, current factors suggest that Sri Lanka will go with the Beijing option. This will provide China with a much larger Sri Lankan presence that will make India comfortable. India could consider including Sri Lankan projects within the infrastructural thrust of India's latest five-year plan. This push would technically come under the heading of fisheries, maritime, and trade development, instead of strategy and security.

An expanding Chinese presence could cause the U.S. to deepen its footprint in the region. Irrespective of the human rights criticism, the U.S. will be compelled to find a balance between strategic and value-based interests. U.S. strategic interests revolve around piracy, protection of SLOCs, and containing China's growing influence. However, because the U.S. was a vociferous critic of the LTTE war's last phase, it may not be in a good position to significantly improve its ties with Sri Lanka. The U.S. could perhaps find alternative ways to achieve its objectives in Sri Lanka. For instance, Israel and/or Japan—a major arms supplier and donor, respectively—could seek to consolidate Sri Lanka ties.

Pakistan-Sri Lanka relations are also emerging as a cause of concern because Islamabad's engagement may not necessarily be in Indian interests. Reports of increasing radicalisation on the eastern border, radicalism fuelled by Pakistan and Saudi Arabia, add to these concerns. For instance, Mirza Himayat Baig, the suspect in the Pune Bakery terror attack, reportedly received training from terror group LeT in Sri Lanka.[146] There are also

[146] "Zaby's arrest boost to Bakery blast probe," *The Indian Express*, June 26, 2012, available at http://www.indianexpress.com/news/zabys-arrest-boost-to-bakery-blast-probe/966808/0.

recent terror attacks in India, whose origins are traceable back to South India, especially Kerala. Given its geographic proximity, radicalisation of eastern Sri Lanka poses a clear danger from terrorism. Sri Lanka's inexperience with Islamic radicalisation and terrorism makes it particularly vulnerable.

Lastly, while Iran-Sri Lanka relations in their present form do not threaten Indian security, new dynamics in India-Iran relations and growing synergy between Tehran and Beijing make this a bilateral relationship to watch. Relations could evolve in a manner not helpful to India's interests, although deepening India-Iran relations over issues like Afghanistan could swing the pendulum in a positive direction.

INDIA'S POLITICAL TIES WITH COLOMBO

India's commitment to the sovereignty, unity, and integrity of Sri Lanka—a commitment shown in its restrained reaction to Sri Lanka's LTTE offensive, despite its human rights implications—helped build much-needed common ground for rebuilding trust. The non-intervention approach was the surest sign to Colombo of India's desire to strengthen the bilateral relationship. Despite this show of good faith, the Geneva vote has done considerable damage to relations with Colombo.

Other divergences appear to be gaining prominence. Three tenets of reconciliation are: one, humanitarian assistance to Tamils in northern and eastern Sri Lanka; two, the reconstruction and rehabilitation of IDPs; and three, political devolution leading to negotiation between Tamil parties and the Sri Lankan government. Though official statements from both India and Sri Lanka indicate convergence on these issues, the urgency shown by India on the underlying concerns remains unmatched by Sri Lanka.

With the LTTE defeat, India can push the Sri Lankan government on Tamil reconciliation without being accused of supporting the LTTE. India also has the opportunity to build credibility among the Tamils by undertaking development work. However, this should be done with caution because India should avoid being seen as pro-Tamil by the majority Sinhala community.

With the government wiping out the LTTE and winning a military victory on the ethnic question, it is felt that Tamil political reconciliation is likely to be a slower process. The Tamils have less leverage since the voice from the North and East has lost intensity. However, losing momentum on resettlement policy and political devolution remains a real danger. This must be avoided, despite compelling geopolitical imperatives. The development agenda must be pursued with a single focus in order to emerge as advantageous for all parties.

The rights of Indian fishermen have also become a point of contention in the recent years. New Delhi reacted strongly to the alleged killing by Sri Lanka's Navy of Indian fishermen venturing into Sri Lankan waters. India's Foreign Secretary visited Sri Lanka to discuss the issue, and the Joint Working Group (JWG) on Fisheries stressed that the international maritime boundary was to be respected. However, the JWG also agreed that the "use of force cannot be justified under any circumstances."[146a]

INDIAN RECONSTRUCTION EFFORTS

The residual Tamil population's reaction to possible calls from the Diaspora Tamils will depend on the pace and pattern of reconstruction and reconciliation process by the Sri Lankan government. Four years after the war, there is some recognition of Sri Lanka's rehabilitation efforts at both the international level and within the Tamil polity (including the TNA). Reconstruction efforts involve medium- and long-term planning and the use of massive resources, which Sri Lanka cannot provide on its own. India has been supportive in this regard, assisting Sri Lanka in rehabilitation and reconstruction. These efforts are in addition to

[146a]Ministry of External Affairs, "Meeting of the India-Sri Lanka JWG on Fisheries–Joint Press Statement," March 29, 2011, available at mea.gov.in/.

pushing Colombo and the TNA to revive political negotiations for a solution acceptable to all sections of Sri Lankan society.

India has given significant assistance in the post-war rehabilitation of the war-torn Tamil areas of the North and East. Additionally, India also extended developmental assistance to projects in other parts of the country. Currently, this contribution includes immediate post-war relief in the form of dry rations, housing material (like zinc-sheet for roofing), and kitchen vessels. The impact of this aid was immediate. Subsequently, reconstruction of war-damaged roads and rail links, aimed at re-linking northern Jaffna to Colombo, has been pursued. Additionally, India undertook restoration of destroyed schools and hospital buildings, rebuilding of Kankesanthurai Port, construction of a Tamil cultural centre at Jaffna, and expanding Jaffna University and hospital facilities in the North and East. India also donated agriculture equipment (including tractors), bicycles for student transport, and committed aid for Tamil deep-sea fishing. The Tamils were left out of deep-sea fishing opportunities during the war years. The main plank of Indian aid for war victims is the construction of 50,000 (and possibly more) housing units.[147] These efforts are aimed at restoring the pre-war livelihood and lifestyles of the Tamil population to whatever degree possible.

India also has a special programme for equipping war-affected women, aimed at acquiring skills to help augment family incomes. Sri Lanka puts the number of Tamil war widows as high as 90,000,[148] with no clear figures on orphaned children, dependent elders or disabled people. There is much India can help with in the coming decades. Immediately after the war's conclusion, Indian medical teams scoured the area for disabled persons to be fitted

[147]Ministry of External Affiants, Government of India, "India-Sri Lanka Bilateral Relations," available at http://meaindia.nic.in/mystart.php?id=50044525.

[148]Sri Lankan government officials admit this only in private discussions.

with the famous 'Jaipur foot,' making them mobile and independent again.[149] In the final months of war, Indian armed forces ran medical camps for victims, first in the Eastern Province and later in the North. Considering the lack of access among Sri Lanka's Tamils to higher education, India should make special efforts to address aspirations in this regard, although these efforts should be structured in a way to avoid 'brain drain' in areas desperately in need of well-educated persons.

The Indian government's resolve, both the central and Tamil Nadu political parties, have driven the Indian policy, with substantial assistance for war victims. Additionally, Sri Lanka has discouraged other nations and U.N. agencies from working in war-affected areas. However, Sri Lanka has enough pragmatism to recognise that it needs assistance from all sources. Accordingly, the U.S., Germany, Norway, Japan, and others started funding specific projects in the North and the East. The first non-Indian nation to do this was China, which has built, with Chinese labour, roads and houses in the Northern and Eastern Provinces.

However, if Sri Lanka relaxes provisions on foreign and U.N. assistance, the possibility of their combined funding outstripping India's contributions will become a reality. India's desire to provide development assistance cannot match the potential firepower of the international community, especially considering China's interest. Meanwhile, if the U.S. and European economic problems continue, these countries will have no choice but to reduce contributions to Sri Lanka's development. China's massive resources and its ability to roll out assistance with no strings attached (i.e., accountability on human rights and war crimes) mean that it may become the country's largest donor.

Potential assistance should not be limited to economic aid but it should also involve infrastructure development. While India has

[149] "Second Jaipur Foot Artificial Limb Fitment Camp Organized in Sri Lanka," *Asian Tribune*, October 05, 2010, available at http://www.asiantribune. com/news/ 2011/10/04/second-jaipur-foot-artificial-limb-fitment-camp-organized-sri-lanka.

undertaken work on a rail-link in the Sinhala South, China already delivered on the Hambantota Port and is working quickly on Mattala International Airport. Although the economic usefulness of India's assistance cannot be questioned, the fast execution of these two projects by China explains why Sri Lankan officials prefer Beijing over New Delhi. Japan maintains involvement in major projects, including the prestigious Southern National Highway.

While India and China compete to make their presence felt in Sri Lanka, they provide different types of aid. Much of China's aid has been in the form of credit at commercial interest rates, whereas India primarily provides grants or loans expected to be written off as grants at a subsequent date.

However, Sri Lanka has had issues dealing with India. One major irritant has been the bureaucratic delays in clearing projects and funding. President Rajapaksa, among others, has gone on record saying that Indian aid takes a long time to materialise. Possibly learning from their Sri Lanka experience, the Indian government has since created a separate fund with 50,000 crores for aiding developing countries. This programme is to be managed exclusively by the Ministry of External Affairs.

INDIA-SRI LANKA DEFENCE TIES

There was some reticence regarding close military relations because of Indian neutrality towards a purely military solution to the LTTE problem. India believes in tethering this to a political solution.

Historically, India provided training to the Sri Lankan military. Intelligence sharing has also been an area of cooperation. The India-Sri Lanka defence relationship was also built on various service-to-service linkages. The sale of military equipment was suspended in the 1980s, though non-lethal weapons were given to Colombo during the 2000 offensive and thereafter. Offshore patrol vessels provided by India were of considerable utility for Sri

Lanka's LTTE fight, although India again refused to supply combat weapons when Sri Lanka requested them in 2006. However, India agreed to provide ships and defensive equipment, like automatic 40mm L-70 close range anti-aircraft guns and Indra low-flying detection radars. Consequently, Sri Lanka approached China, Israel, Iran, and Pakistan, many of whom were more than willing to provide offensive weapons. These included fighter aircraft, tanks, and UAVs. One of the Chinese arms suppliers, NORINCO, even set up a warehouse in Galle. Sri Lanka was given a line of credit, and its forces were permitted to take warehouse items as and when needed. Lastly, there is a trilateral partnership between Sri Lanka, Pakistan, and China, which may be detrimental to Indian interests. The commonality of defence equipment among these countries has only furthered their defence interactions.

In the absence of a proper reconciliation process, military relations may remain strained. Within India, there may be disagreements between the security and defence agencies and foreign policy and political mainstream, which have different views on strategic engagement with Sri Lanka. This will become all the more important in the present context, with the Indian Ocean increasingly becoming an area of intense military, economic, and diplomatic competition. In this context, a defence cooperation agreement between India and Sri Lanka would go a long way towards guarding India's interests.

The idea of a defence pact was publicly conceived in a 2003 joint statement. The draft cooperation agreement was primarily viewed as an attempt to "regularize existing cooperation"[150] that was already taking place between the two countries. India had been providing Sri Lanka with non-lethal weapons since 2000, so the proposed agreement was seen as a framework under which

[150]"India-Sri Lanka Defence Agreement," OpEd, *The Hindu*, October 26, 2004, available at http://www.hindu.com/2004/10/26/stories/2004102602761000.htm

existing transactions could continue. However, the agreement was not a bilateral defence treaty, which would have allowed Sri Lanka comprehensive access to India's defence equipment and technology.[151]

After preliminary discussions were held during President Kumaratunga's visit to India, the agreement was slated for signing towards the end of 2004.[152] It was to be accompanied by an MoU on joint modernisation of Palaly Air Force Base and Trincomalee Harbour.[153]

However, Sri Lankan analysts expressed scepticism, suggesting that India remained reluctant to engage further because of the IPKF experience.[154] Political issues posed by Tamil Nadu political parties were also seen as an obstacle. However, media reports suggest that the disagreement was over MoU provisions, rather than the Defence Cooperation Agreement (DCA).[155] There was a failure to agree on joint use of two airports near Jaffna and the Trincomalee Harbour. India sought exclusive use, while Sri Lanka wished to keep it open to other countries. Then Sri Lankan Foreign Minister Laxman Kadirgamar reportedly said that the agreement was complete except for a single clause.[156]

After the war, even as some analysts called for expediting defence cooperation, others suggested that ground realities already indicated substantial cooperation. They believe the new framework would only formalise the cooperation, while also

[151] *ibid.*

[152] "India, Sri Lanka working on defence pact: Kumaratunga," *The Indian Express*, January 08, 2004, available at http://www.indianexpress.com/oldStory/38784/.

[153] Saji Cherian, "Tilting the Balance," *South Asia Intelligence Review*, Vol. 3, No. 18, 15 November 2004.

[154] Ranjit Devraj, "India Defensive Over Sri Lanka," Institute of Policy Studies, Sri Lanka, November 16, 2004.

[155] Sugeeswara Senadhira, "Hitch in Indo-Lanka Defence Pact," *Asian Tribune*, May 04, 2005, available at http://www.asiantribune.com/news/2005/05/04/hitch-indo-lanka-defence-pact.

[156] *ibid.*

increasing tensions. Instead, it was argued that long-term work plan should be carried out, working towards a basic framework agreement to enhance existing cooperation.

Looking ahead, India must pursue a strengthened maritime cooperation that ensures Sri Lankan strategic autonomy and facilitates an orderly reorientation of Indian Ocean dynamics. One possibility is building a strong Sri Lankan navy, a project in which India should be an active partner.

INDIA'S ECONOMIC INTERESTS IN SRI LANKA

Bilateral economic engagement has been heralded as the hallmark of India-Sri Lanka relations. The liberalisation of the Indian economy in 1991 gave impetus for an increase in trade and investment. Since the early 1990s, trade figures have increased exponentially, doubling from 1993 to 1996 and again increasing manifold since the signing of the Indo-Sri Lanka Free Trade Agreement (ISLFTA) in 1998.[157] The ISLFTA significantly improved trade relations and helped reduce the import-export ratio imbalance, which until then was grossly tilted towards India.

The Sri Lankan political class has long been suspicious of India's dominance in their economic relations. Many even vehemently opposed the Comprehensive Economic Partnership Agreement (CEPA), which was meant to tackle the problems with the FTA and enhance bilateral trade relations. However, these suspicions can be overcome with time and a commitment to all-round engagement and mutual development, ensuring the security of both Indian and Sri Lankan economic interests.

The future of India-Sri Lanka economic relations is dependent on the continuation of current trade and also the identification of new avenues for engagement. This would ideally include the

[157]Orland, Brian, "India's Sri Lanka Policy: Towards Economic Engagement," *IPCS Research Papers No. 16*, Institute of Peace and Conflict Studies, April 2008, available at http://www.ipcs.org/pdf_file/issue/1445888596RP16-Brian-SriLanka.pdf.

energy sector, particularly offshore oil exploration in the Mannar basin. India would also be interested in business opportunities to emerge in the North, as it regains stability. Indian companies have also established a reasonably strong investment presence in Sri Lanka, including FDI approvals of nearly U.S. $500 million. India was Sri Lanka's largest FDI source in 2010, contributing U.S. $110 million out of the U.S. $516 million received in total. For India, it is imperative to maintain and continue building the preferential advantage it presently enjoys in Sri Lankan economic circles. Chinese and Pakistani economic interests could, however, pose a looming threat. While Sri Lanka has thus far maintained diplomatic and strategic balance in its external economic engagement, India must enhance relations in order to avoid any future hiccups. Fisheries are also likely to become a major aspect of cooperation between the two sides, especially because Sri Lankan waters offer lucrative fishing zones.

Arrangements for credit, loans, rebuilding, and reconstruction are already in place. A line of credit of U.S. $167.4 million for upgrading the Colombo-Matara rail link and another U.S. $800 million for Northern railway line were announced in June 2010. Another agreement for a credit line of U.S. $416.39 million was signed in November 2010 to support construction of Medawachchiya to Madhu, Madhu to Talaimannar, and Omanthai to Pallai railway lines in Northern Sri Lanka. Ensuring connectivity and undertaking massive infrastructure projects should be a priority while looking at economic development. Additionally, IRCON International Limited's visible presence in constructing such infrastructure could engender regional goodwill toward India.[158]

Important infrastructure-related projects currently under discussion include the 500 MW coal-based power plant in Trincomalee and inter-connectivity between the Indian and Sri

[158]IRCON is a government company incorporated by the Ministry of Railways, Government of India.

Lankan electricity grids. India is also assisting in the restoration of Kankesanthurai Harbour and the development of Palaly Airfield as a civil airport. Building of port infrastructure should be taken up as a priority.

Meanwhile, there is always fear within the Sri Lankan government that India's northern and eastern reconstruction projects will enable New Delhi to reap undue goodwill among the Tamil community. Sri Lanka fears the Tamils could pose a threat to the state's stability in the event of a Tamil militancy revival. Having a powerful, influential Tamil group in Sri Lanka could be in India's interest if and when they attain power.

In the medium to long term, India should push for a formal conclusion of the CEPA based on a few key parameters: expansion of trade (including services), boosting investments, and diversifying into various sectors—such as transportation, infrastructure, and Information and Communication Technology. India should push for port development, especially of Trincomalee, as well as for an on-site oil storage facility. The two countries have already resumed CEPA discussions, including steps to finalise the agreement. However, there are some obstacles remaining, including difficulty in licensing procedure, high license fees, shortage of local skills, import restrictions, and problems with professional regulatory bodies in Sri Lanka.

India's economic interests include extending Indian service sector expertise to Sri Lanka, especially for boosting its health and education sector. Considerable efforts should be devoted towards resolving non-tariff barrier issues and service agreement safeguards to guard against Sri Lankan vulnerabilities. Cooperation in oil and gas sector may get a boost, especially from the Mannar basin area.

In the longer term, a massive east-west dedicated freight corridor linking Trincomalee-Vavuniya-Talaimannar-Ramanathapuram should be constructed. The year 2014 will mark 50 years since a cyclone washed away the railway line linking the small pilgrimage town of Dhanushkodi and Rameswaram. This could become a good commemorative beginning. This project would ensure direct, visible Indian access to the Trincomalee Port, while also facilitating a developmental corridor on either side of the freight line.

Sri Lanka remains India's largest trade partner in SAARC, while India is Sri Lanka's largest single country trading partner globally. Between 2000 and 2010, total bilateral trade increased from under U.S. $50 million to nearly U.S. $2 billion. An Indian Council for Research on International Economic Relations (ICRIER) study notes that inclusion of services in CEPA could give the pact an even greater wallop. The study further suggests the scope of Indian investments be increased to include telecommunications, construction, and oil. Indian oil and gas companies should look to expand their operations to Sri Lanka.

CULTURAL TIES

India is the linguistic and religious birthplace of the Sinhala and Tamil beliefs systems. Buddhism grew slowly in India until the reign of Mauryan Emperor Ashoka. During Ashoka's time, emissaries travelled the Silk Road to China and throughout South and Southeast Asia, spreading religion.[159] Recorded history shows that Mahinda, son and disciple of Emperor Ashoka, converted the Sri Lankan King Devanampiya Tissa to Buddhism in 267 B.C. Similarly, Hinduism spilled out from Indian shores. The Tamil language originated in India, while Sinhala bears a close resemblance to the Brahmi script-based 'Vattezhuthu,' which was a forerunner to languages like Kerala's Malayalam. Buddhism was nearly extinct in India by the late middle ages, although it is today regaining strength.[160]

Understanding the historical and socio-cultural moorings of Sri Lanka is key to deciphering the growing cultural ties between

[159] "Buddhism," 2009, in Encyclopedia Britannica, Retrieved on November 26, 2009, from *Encyclopedia Britannica Online Library Edition*.

[160] Carol E. Henderson, *Culture and Customs of India* (Greenwood Publishing Group, 2002, p. 42. Also see Joseph B. Tamney in William H. Swatos (ed.), *Encyclopedia of Religion and Society*, Rowman Altamira, 1998, p. 68.

these nations. India alone can claim such a vast cultural overlap with the island.

The Sinhala civilisation's history is recounted originally in the Mahavamsa, the greatest Pali chronicle of Sri Lanka. Sinhala mythology alludes to the idea that Sinhalese are the supposed guardians of Buddhist teachings. The Sinhalese believe that Prince Vijaya and his Aryan followers came from Sinhapura (now Bengal) to Sri Lanka on the day of Buddha's death. This event marked the beginning of Sinhala civilisation. The Mahavamsa portrays Hindu Tamils as invaders, symbolised by King Elara's occupation of Anuradhapura. His defeat at the hands of Prince Dutugemunu in the 2nd century BC remains an epic event and cause for celebration in the Sinhala tradition. Subsequent invasions, like those by the Cholas from Tamil Nadu, reinforced the idea of the Tamil invader. Due to periodic invasions from South India, the Sinhalese tend to affiliate more with Northern India.

Sinhala views acquired racial overtones during the regime of Anagarika Dharmapala (1864-1933). His reign reinforced their self-perception as the original inhabitants of Sri Lanka, keepers of the Buddhist faith and chosen rulers of the island. Tamils question these claims based on their Yalpanna Vaipava Malai text. Tamils believe their settlements predate the Sinhala arrival. Given Tamil numerical majority just across the Palk Strait and their established historic, linguistic, and cultural legacy, the Sinhalese harbour an acute minority consciousness and cultural inferiority complex. These disputes and insecurities lie at the heart of Sinhala-Tamil antagonism.

Modern Sri Lanka and India share a common cultural heritage, which can provide avenues for greater cultural cooperation. However, such cooperation has been largely limited to Buddhist institutions, like the Mahabodhi society.[161] Other

[161]Mahabodhi Society of Sri Lanka, Buddhist Theosophical Society (at Adiyar) have been founded by Col. Olcott.

ventures have often been individual, rather than institution-driven. The upswing seen during the tenure of Sri Lankan Foreign Minister Laxman Kadirgamar is a case in point.[162] New directions could be taken by exploring Theravada (prominent in Sri Lanka) school's influence on Dalit Buddhism (founded by BR Ambedkar). However, even these Buddhist connections are tenuous, as Mahayana Buddhism has predominated in India.[163] A recent endeavour to rediscover Nalanda has essentially commemorated the Mahayana centre of learning.[164]

Leveraging Buddhism to improve relations with Sri Lanka would ideally begin with a focus on the Theravada School, which could be done by banking on Ambedkar's legacy. Combined with caste movements, this is a social problem which is common to both Indian and Sri Lankan society. However, for caste-sensitive Tamils, Ambedkar (who stood for upliftment of backward sections of the society in India) is unlikely to be viewed with antagonism, providing the much-needed common ground.

On the other hand, the Mahayana and Theravada schools have a common origin. Vinaya Pitaka and the four principal Nikayas or Agamas underlie all Buddhist teachings. If common ground can facilitate the convergence of both schools, then initiatives like Nalanda University (originally based on the Mahayana School of thought) can be combined with the Theravada School in order to strengthen bilateral cultural and religious bonds.

Blavatsky and Olcott's attempts at creating a Buddhist theosophical society in India, and later Sri Lanka, based on the idea of universal brotherhood should also be viewed as one possible pillar on which to build institutional cooperation.

[162]Discussion with Prof. Sudharshan Seneviratne, University of Peridanya, Sri Lanka.

[163]Oldest form literally meaning "Elders school," closest in resemblance to the original thought of the Buddha.

[164]"Vision for a New Nalanda," Interview with Amartya Sen, *The Hindu*, September 19, 2011, available at http://www.thehindu.com/opinion/interview/article2465374.ece.

India must ensure a renewed emphasis on ancient Buddhist ties between the Sinhalese and India's northern and eastern regions. If successful, this may offset to some degree the widely held Sinhalese perception of Indian interests as too convergent with those of Hindu Tamils in Sri Lanka. Socio-cultural cooperation is one limited way in which India can (and should) engage the Sinhalese majority.

There is an increasing rivalry between India and China for influence even in the Buddhist domain. India has gone the extra mile to draw attention to its 'solid Buddhist credentials,' emphasising Buddhism's Indian origins around 5th century BC. Only afterwards did it spread across Asia to countries such as Sri Lanka, Nepal, Bhutan, Myanmar, Thailand, Vietnam, Laos, Cambodia, Japan, Korea, Tibet, Mongolia, and China. India must proactively work this 'soft power' angle in its diplomacy, particularly when dealing with Sri Lanka.

A multinational effort with countries including India, China, and Japan is now spearheading the Nalanda Initiative. India is at the centre of the effort as a university is being set up—Nalanda International University. However, China wants to ensure its links to the university are not forgotten. China is part of a mentor group, headed by Nobel laureate Amartya Sen, providing vision and direction to the Nalanda Initiative. Additionally, China contributed funds for the university's Xuan Zang Memorial Hall, ensuring that its Buddhist links are noted.

The vistas of cultural cooperation are widespread, from religious to linguistic. These range from eastern India-Sinhala cooperation based on a shared heritage and religious tradition to Tamil Nadu-Tamil cooperation on music, dance, and arts. Building such ties remains an ongoing process. The limits to cultural cooperation lie with inherent non-acceptance of multiculturalism within Sri Lankan society. There is an urgent need to discover a common cultural platform for Indo-Sri Lankan cooperation, rather than piecemeal Indo-Tamil or Indo-Sinhala links. This sort of cooperation could enhance ties even if limited in nature.

Other groupings, such as the National Commission on Minority Rights and National Commission on Scheduled Castes and Tribes, should be encouraged to share experiences on minority empowerment. Among extra-constitutional bodies, the Planning Commission could be encouraged to present the processes used to develop India's long-term plans.

A more value-based, normative foreign policy could reflect India's civilisational and cultural beliefs. A shift in this direction could promote and prioritise a greater display of Indian values. These could be expanded by funding more cultural centres and promoting Indian art, dance, and music.

Finally, soft power in the form of aid and loans may have a more visible, tangible impact on Indo-Sri Lanka relations. Although it will be difficult to compete with China in terms of economic resources at its disposal, India could draw on its geographic and cultural advantages in a much more systematic manner. India must focus on the quality and impact of its investments to ensure significant soft power returns.

Despite the delicate India-Sri Lanka balancing act that has taken place after the Geneva vote, the relationship between the two countries has a huge growth potential. The Geneva vote cannot be allowed to dictate a negative direction in the relationship. With the conclusion of the Eelam War, India must find ways to open a multiple-front cooperative framework with Sri Lanka.

VIII

Conclusion

The three-decade long ethnic conflict in Sri Lanka, which ended in May 2009, offers both challenges and opportunities for Colombo and New Delhi. The two sides can help engender a successful national reconstruction in Sri Lanka while also reforming and redefining bilateral relations. Such achievements could also precipitate significant peace dividends for future generations. For this to occur, Sri Lanka's leadership must address the legitimate aspirations of its Tamil community, various internal contradictions, and the likely emergence of the Muslim community as a viable party in the nation's politics.

While Sri Lanka's military played a pivotal role in the Eelam War, its basic role and approach have remained unchanged even in the post-war scenario. The military has, by and large, maintained its apolitical nature, ensuring balance in civil-military relations. In the few instances when military officials took political positions, they did so only after retirement from active service. However, the military and nation will be challenged by post-war demobilisation of a particularly large army. Finding alternate employment will remain difficult.

In the post-war era, Sri Lanka will need sustained economic growth to meet the growing aspirations of its citizens, to reconstruct war-torn areas and to realise its goal of becoming the 'hub' of South Asia. These economic compulsions will likely drive Colombo's internal and external policies.

In the backdrop of rapidly changing geopolitical dynamics in the Asia-Pacific region—including the rise of China and increasing major power rivalries in IOR—Sri Lanka's strategic location gives the country an added significance for major power strategy and leverage in negotiations over various issues.

Sri Lanka assumes particular importance in India's foreign policy. A peaceful immediate neighbourhood is essential if India is to emerge as a global power. Sri Lanka is important to neighbourhood stability and presents a classic case of domestic politics influencing Indian foreign policy. In any case, India's aspirations are tied to both Sri Lanka's security and the nature of its relationships with foreign powers.

POLITICAL, ETHNO-RELIGIOUS, AND DEMOGRAPHIC ISSUES

The Sri Lankan political landscape is undergoing changes, with elitist domination giving way to a more pluralistic representation. Although caste and class continue to be significant determinants at the national political scene, there has been substantial improvement in regional and caste representation. These new dynamics and the weakening of the two dominant political parties have contributed to the rise of coalition politics. This trend is likely to continue.

After LTTE was defeated, the Tamils voice has, to a large extent, lost its impact in Sri Lankan politics. However, with the emergence of coalition politics, Sri Lankan Tamil parties can regain a certain degree of influence in the national political scene. A demographic shift favouring Muslim population in the Eastern Province indicates that domination of Muslims in the minority political scene in the future is likely. This will come at the expense of other ethnic groups, particularly the SLTs and IOTs. These are not options wherein India's interests would be adversely affected. In fact, India could inject a positive approach particularly in the economic and strategic realms and emerge as a staying power.

Finding a solution to Sri Lanka's ethnic issues and bringing the Tamil minority into the mainstream should be important goals for the country's leadership. The challenges are many. They include changing the socio-political, economic and ethnic fabric of society by increasing Tamil representation at the political, educational, military, and bureaucratic arenas. At the same time, a possible resurgence of Tamil militancy must be guarded against. The pace and direction of ethnic reconciliation depends on the government's deftness in handling these issues and balancing the competing challenges. Thus far, government efforts in this regard seem inadequate.

SOCIO-ECONOMIC AND COMMERCIAL ISSUES

The Sri Lankan economy has seen increasing GDP growth in recent years. While Sri Lanka recorded the highest growth rate in South Asia in 2010 (8 per cent), internal and external constraints to growth persist. These obstacles must be given due consideration when analysing Sri Lanka's future.

After identifying the service sector as key to growth, the government took steps to make services exportable and resistant to international competition. *Mahinda Chinatana*, which shapes current government policies, focuses primarily on developing services in the port, aviation, energy, knowledge, and commercial (including trading and banking and finance) industries. These initiatives indicate that the already prospering service sector will further improve and potentially bolster the country's economy.

However, the upward shift of Sri Lanka's economy will be restricted unless its demographic challenges are addressed. Studies reflect how women are fast outpacing working-age men. Unfortunately, much of this female labour force remains unemployed. Furthermore, the agricultural sector's meagre GDP contribution compared to the percentage of people it employs reflects a need to better utilise Sri Lanka's workforce.

Externally, Sri Lanka's diminished global image may eventually have significantly adverse consequences on its economy. The UNHRC resolutions condemning Sri Lanka for human rights abuses highlights its falling reputation. India, which was Sri Lanka's second largest source of 2010 foreign finance, also backed the resolution. While the resolution is unlikely to alter short-run foreign investments and assistance, Sri Lanka will need to ensure effective implementation of the 'Lessons Learnt and Reconciliation Commission' recommendations if it wants to maintain the long-term flow of external assistance and funding.

Continued service sector development and foreign assistance will drive Sri Lanka's GDP growth. The potential social impact of enhanced government revenue will depend upon the government's ability to effectuate better disbursement of wealth. Although Sri Lanka's economic situation has improved in recent years, several obstacles stand in the way of its ambitions to become another Singapore by 2025.

GEOPOLITICAL AND STRATEGIC ISSUES

Sri Lanka occupies a unique geostrategic position in the Indian Ocean region, which makes it attractive to most regional powers. Changing geostrategic dynamics in the IOR give Sri Lanka significant leverage. China has come a long way in wooing Indian Ocean littoral states, using strategic and financial investments and concessional development loans. China-Sri Lanka growing bonhomie raises concerns for India. China's increased IOR presence raises the possibility that other powers like the U.S. will increase engagement with Colombo in a balancing manoeuvre.

Given its geographically advantageous position vis-à-vis international shipping, Colombo plans to develop its port infrastructure, along with air, road, and rail projects to strengthen regional connectivity. These moves show the country's growing desire to emerge as a major regional shipping hub, which will only attract other major players to strengthen their foothold in the island nation.

If it does not tread carefully, Colombo will likely find itself at the centre of conflicting major power interests. Sri Lanka must craft a foreign policy that balances these conflicting interests. Colombo's ability to achieve this balance will determine its role in the emerging geopolitics of the IOR. It remains likely that China-Sri Lanka relations will only strengthen in the future, giving Colombo a (China) card to balance India when it is in their interests. However, given its proximity to India and New Delhi's rising geopolitical and military power, Colombo needs to restrain itself from crossing any red lines.

Given the internal and external factors influencing Sri Lanka, India must institute policies that ensure its sovereignty and integrity while also promoting economic integration and limiting the adverse (to India's interests) impact of external players. India's policy should be guided by growing maritime and energy security interests, which would lead to a more pragmatic approach toward Sri Lanka. This course correction would rectify some of the recent pitfalls that have negatively coloured the relationship.

IX

Trends and Scenarios for Sri Lanka 2025

While there could be several different scenarios that may emerge depending on a combination of factors, this report outlines three distinct scenarios for Sri Lanka and Indo-Sri Lanka relations in 2025. These were developed analysing four major factors: ethno-religious; political and demographic; socio-economic and commercial; and geopolitical and strategic drivers.

Scenario I: Most likely

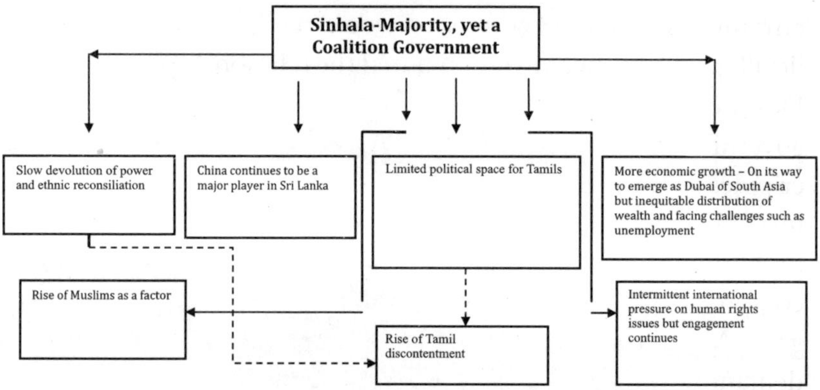

Scenario I: Sinhala-Majority, yet Coalition Government

In this scenario, Sri Lankan politics most closely resembles the current configuration in Colombo. Major political parties, such as the SLFP and UNP, continue to dominate Parliament. No other political party, alliance of political parties, or extra-electoral institutions dislodge the traditional power centres. The 'relatively moderate mainstream' political parties dominate Sri Lankan politics and prevent radical groups from gaining ground through elections.

Notwithstanding the enduring prominence of major parties, none are able to claim a majority on their own and must instead rely on a host of smaller parties to form a coalition government. Hence, incumbent governments comprised one of the main national parties, supported by a group of smaller parties, resembling the Indian political situation.

Sri Lankan coalition politics engenders limited ethnic minority representation, especially of the Tamil community. In fact, following the culmination of war against LTTE and subsequent international criticism, Colombo makes efforts to promote Tamil political leadership as part of a strategy to prevent the return of militant violence.

However, the emergence of new, potent political parties is circumvented by an absence of capacity-building and development in Tamil majority regions of northern Sri Lanka. Despite verbal assurances, successive Sinhalese-dominated governments avoid the important issue of power devolution. This cripples the development of grassroots, local-level politics and instead encourages patronage. A crisis of political legitimacy prevails because most locals believe Tamil politicians compromised the community's interests in favour of personal gain. Moreover, Colombo's complete insensitivity towards the demand for a 'truth and reconciliation' process to probe wanton human rights abuses only further alienates the Tamil community. Efforts, however insincere, at political representation are completely quashed and Tamil discontentment is further fuelled.

As for Sri Lanka's external relations, two features are defining. First, China's role is ever increasing. Second, recurrent international criticism of the country's human rights record hampers development.

Balancing the interests of major players—including China, India, the U.S., and other western powers—remains the most pressing concern of Colombo's foreign policy. The West engages with Colombo, even as it continues to pressure Sri Lanka on the Tamil issue. Mutually beneficial ties between China and Sri Lanka continue. Sino-Sri Lanka economic ties further expand to serve Sri Lanka's internal needs and Western countries remain ambivalent towards full-spectrum engagement with Colombo owing to lack of progress on ethnic reconciliation.

Sri Lanka's economy registers impressive growth as it marches closer to its Dubai or Singapore-like potential. Its ports attract greater percentages of global maritime traffic. Relaxed regulations make it a new tourism hub for South Asians, where it competes with Singapore and Thailand as an affordable destination. However, like many other developing countries, glitzy malls and skyscrapers do not ensure a 'trickling down' of wealth. Most Sri Lankans remain outside the growth bubble, as unequal wealth distribution and lack of access to government-related perks and opportunities plague the country.

Ethnic reconciliation remains a key factor shaping this scenario. Resolving this problem (or not) seriously impacts the internal political situation and determines, to an extent, Colombo's external engagements. While ethnic harmony continues to create both internal and external challenges for the Sri Lankan government, many other factors are likely to remain unchanged in the near term (next decade or so).

No major LTTE-like militant group challenges state sovereignty and there is minimal possibility of fringe groups mobilising into a potent threat, given the devastating impact of the war on the Tamils and the heavy government militarisation of the northern and eastern regions. As a result, the country is unlikely to witness a major armed ethnic conflict in the near future. The Sri Lankan government has the ability to nip nascent militancy in the bud.

Externally, the country faces diplomatic challenges episodically over the issue of human rights violations during the last stages of civil war and the need to speed up ethnic reconciliation. However, this international attention does not cause serious political or economic crises. Geopolitical rivalries and strategic compulsions ensure that Sri Lanka always has some international backing, a tremendous source of leverage for Colombo.

Demographic changes mean increased clout for Sri Lanka's Muslim community. This will alter the political calculus among ethnic minorities. In particular, this causes significant shifts in local Eastern Province politics where the Muslim community has emerged in large numbers. Also, the government's concerns regarding the threat of militant Islam and its linkages to global terrorism are amplified.

By 2025, military expenditure will begin to decline. This will enable Colombo to divert resources to sectors such as healthcare, agriculture and northeast socio-economic development. Pensions and healthcare expenditure are likely to increase given the population age structure. The degree of development in the North and East depends on policy options adopted by the government. Unfortunately, it continues to neglect regions previously affected by militancy.

Scenario II: Less likely but ideal for India

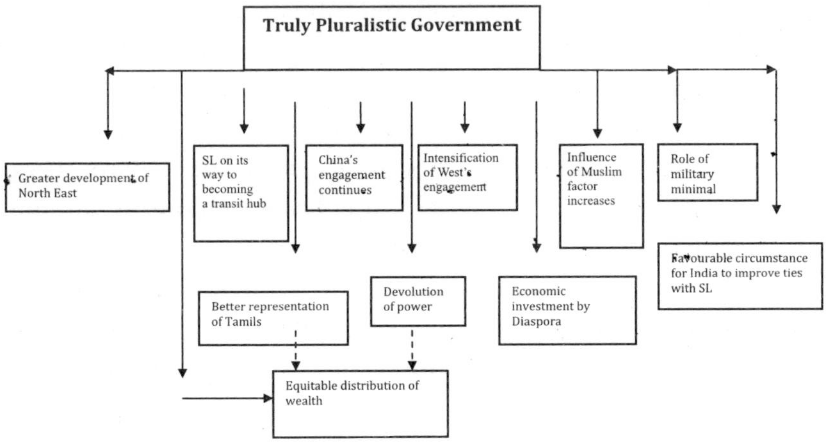

SCENARIO II: A PLURALISTIC SRI LANKAN GOVERNMENT

Political, ethno-religious and demographic factors determine this scenario. This situation occurs when Sri Lanka's ethnic and religious minorities obtain an equal political platform and emerge as influential parties in Sri Lankan society. Additionally, they are better represented in government, including the bureaucracy and military.

Two primary factors give this scenario shape. First, current and successive governments in Colombo succumb to international pressure, making serious efforts at ethnic reconciliation and also addressing minority grievances by ensuring a political voice, equal opportunity in education, and employment and development in the North and East. Second, the emergence of coalition politics allows minority parties to gain national influence, an influence felt beyond their native region.

International pressure continues to build on Sri Lanka's government, ultimately forcing Colombo to address the Tamil issue and devolve power. The Muslim community's rise, as highlighted in earlier chapters, forces the government to recognise the group's growing demands and aspirations. The twin threats of radicalisation and Islamic terrorism motivate Colombo to maintain positive engagement with the community and its political leaders. Reconstruction and infrastructure development programmes in the North and East improve substantially. These developments further enable more equitable distribution of wealth, benefitting all sections of the society.

Therefore, coalition politics in a pluralistic environment generates a security policy rooted in political empowerment and development, rather than force and attrition.

Sri Lanka's 'velvet glove' approach to internal security reduces the need for a strong, inward-looking military. The government downsizes the army, establishing primacy of civilian state institutions and eliminating fears of a post-war coup d'etat.

However, this also presents a new challenge of providing ex-servicemen with benefits and alternate employment.

Colombo's plans to exploit its strategic IOR location allow the Sri Lankan economy to continue its remarkable growth. This enables the government to allocate increased funds for developing the Northern and Eastern Provinces. Good governance and a business-friendly environment encourage the Tamil Diaspora to invest in Sri Lanka.

Sri Lanka's aggressive efforts to become a major transit point for international shipping, presenting a cheaper alternative to Singapore, are noticed by the international community. Increased economic importance and growing strategic IOR competition make Sri Lanka an increasingly important factor in the superpower calculus. Colombo's adherence to human rights values generates U.S. and E.U. interest, prompting both to engage more proactively. Simultaneously, China increases engagement with Colombo by focussing on transit infrastructure. However, an emerging balance of power between China, India, and a host of western powers proscribes Chinese military ambitions in Sri Lanka. India continues to maintain a position of primacy.

Scenario III: Unlikely and not desirable for India

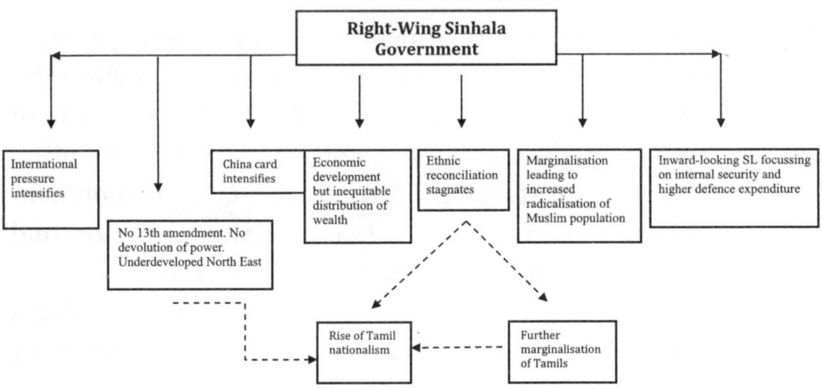

SCENARIO III: MAJORITARIAN SINHALA GOVERNMENT

Sri Lankan society and government continue with post-war triumphalism, failing to distinguish between the LTTE and the larger Tamil community. As a result, Sinhala-majority parties harden their stance against minority communities. Exaggerated and often imagined fears of an LTTE-like group resurgence allows this government to adopt informal policies subjugating Tamil and Muslim society, curtailing many fundamental rights and creating an environment of fear and insecurity of state coercion.

The ethnic reconciliation process stagnates, further marginalising the Tamil community. Devolution of power and 13th Amendment implementation remain unlikely and distant. Government insecurity toward minorities alienates the Muslim population as well. Also, development efforts in the North and East progress slowly.

Continued deprivation of ethnic minorities at a time when post-war reconstruction generates prosperity elsewhere further marginalises these groups. This situation generates Tamil nationalism and radicalisation among the Muslim community. In turn, these developments feed into the government's negative perception of ethnic minorities as a 'security problem,' creating a vicious and self-perpetuating cycle.

Colombo's repressive treatment of Tamils severely curtails India's engagement options, especially regarding high-profile infrastructure projects and investments. The Indian business community is similarly affected, reducing its stakes in the country.

The West remains stuck between advocating for human rights and promoting strategic interests. From Colombo's perspective, the U.S, appears to be fence-sitting. Chinese inroads into Sri Lanka are accelerated by U.S. ambivalence, which is no doubt driven by a strong U.S. human-rights lobby and Washington's tendency to defer its South Asia policy to India. Meanwhile, India continues its traditional stance of remaining sceptical toward a superpower presence on its periphery. The E.U. exerts even greater pressure on Sri Lanka to fulfil its human rights obligations but stops short of calling for international sanctions.

Despite international condemnation, Sri Lanka receives generous support from China. This helps Colombo undermine international demand to develop more equitable socio-economic policies. The government's military-heavy approach to social security puts added pressure on defence expenditure and increases the military's role in policy matters.

Following the conclusion of civil war and subsequent nation-building programmes, China emerges as a prominent player in extending substantial reconstruction aid and securing lucrative infrastructure development projects. It builds a 'world class' international airport, constructs expressways, designs ambitious railways system, and beats out U.S. and South Korean firms for contracts to build Colombo's first underground metro transport system.

Beijing's presence in Sri Lanka is not limited to development. While claiming that China's interests are primarily motivated by businesses interests, increased state visits, army-to-army counter-terrorism exercises and conventional arms purchases certainly alarm India. New Delhi recognises and fears China's ambition to replace India's traditional foothold in Sri Lanka.

The overall geopolitical situation and rising defence budget has a negative impact on Sri Lanka's economy. Foreign investments decrease and despite rising Chinese aid and infrastructure development, the country fails to reach desired rates of economic growth. As a consequence, wealth distribution, access to government services and sustainable development suffer.

Appendix I

Total Population (in multiples of '000)

	2001			2006			2010		
	Total	Male (%)	Female (%)	Total	Male (%)	Female (%)	Total	Male (%)	Female (%)
Central	2,424	49.25	50.7	2,576	49.2	50.8	2,689	49.3	50.7
Eastern	1,419	50.45	**49.5**	1,525	50.5	**49.5**	1,561	48.9	**51.1**
Northern	1,041	-	-	1,111	49.6	**50.4**	1,193	48.6	**51.4**
North Central	1,104	51.4	**48.5**	1,172	51.5	**48.5**	1,240	51.4	**48.6**
North Western	2,170	49.6	50.4	2,266	49.6	50.4	2,342	49.6	50.4
Sabaragamuva	1,802	49.8	50.2	1,884	49.8	50.2	1,943	48.9	50.2
Southern	2,278	48.9	51.09	2,392	48.9	51.1	2,494	48.9	51.1
Western	5,381	49.9	50.1	5,669	49.9	50.1	5,865	49.9	50.1
Uva	1,178	50.2	**49.8**	1,263	50.1	**49.8**	1,326	50.2	**49.8**

Appendix II

Mean Household Income of Provinces

(Note: The value is in SL Rs.)

	2002	2006	2010
Central	11,175	23,875	31,895
Eastern	7,640	20,811*	23,922
Northern	8,155	*	23,712
North Central	**9,926**	**24,759**	**35,577**
North Western	10,918	22,565	35,586
Sabaragamuva	8,439	20,712	36,173
Southern	11,229	24,059	32,514
Western	**17,732**	**34,282**	**47,118**
Uva	**10,388**	**21,371**	**28,717**

* The 2006 survey excludes the Trincomalee district in the Eastern province, and the entire Northern province.

Appendix III
Provinces' Access to Safe Drinking Water (%)

Province	2006	2009
Central	70.6	72.1
Eastern	92.2	89.1
Northern	*	
North Central	**86.4**	**82.7**
North Western	90.5	86.2
Sabaragamuva	67.2	72.9
Southern	84.4	85
Western	94.3	94.4
Uva	**81.4**	**78.3**

Source: UNDP 2005. Millennium Development Goals Country Report: Sri Lanka Data unavailable for Northern Province (Jaffna, Mannar, Vavuniya, Mullaitivu, Kilinochchi)

Index